ONLY BELIEVE

"CHAPTER ONE"

SHANE BAXTER

Shane Baxter

41 Lance Road, Sunshine North VIC 3020, Australia

Shane.Baxter@enjoy.church

First published 2024

Copyright © 2024 Shane Baxter

The moral right of Shane Baxter to be identified as the author of this work has been asserted in accordance with the *Copyright Amendment (Moral Rights) Act 2000*.

All rights reserved. No part of this book may be reproduced or transmitted by any person or entity (including Google, Amazon or similar organisations), in any form or by any means, electronic or mechanical, including photocopying, recording, scanning or by any information storage and retrieval system, without prior permission in writing from the publisher.

ISBN: 978-0-6486286-0-6 (paperback)
       978-0-6486286-1-3 (ebook)

 A catalogue record for this book is available from the National Library of Australia

Edited by Sue Marshall
Cover design by Nico Tapia and Cristian Szust
Text design by Nicole Melbourne
Typeset by Nikki M Group Pty Ltd

*'For My Georgie Girl,
My Faithful & True'*

'ONLY BELIEVE'

Endorsements

I love this man, his ministry, and mission. Pastor Shane Baxter writes, speaks and lives what he believes and preaches because his words are from his heart.

We do not need another expert on life, rather we need a navigator through life. As you read through the chapters, he will take you on a journey of faith and the pursuit for each of us to complete God's destiny for our lives.

I have known Pastor Shane and Georgie since they were praying for their first building. Today they have fifteen locations (and adding more) in three nations with revival every week. Shane pours out his heart, life experiences, God moments, victories and setbacks to write this must-read book—'Only Believe'.

Remember: Jesus never leaves you where he finds you.

GLEN BERTEAU
Founding Pastor of The House Churches

ENDORSEMENTS

I've been blessed reading Shane's book. His warm joyful personality, spiritual sensitivity and faith-filled leadership gift comes through in every chapter. This is the Shane I have known and admired for many of his ministry years as I served with him on both the ACC State and National Executives.

I'm sure Shane's heartwarming openness and faith-building insights will encourage and help you in your own journey of faith. Shane holds nothing back; courageously sharing both his highs and his lows.

In so doing, we are drawn into and benefit from the powerful, practical lessons drawn out of his experiences.

I have always admired Shane's faith and compassion and I am privileged to call him a friend. He has shown himself to be a unique gift to the church. Enjoy Church carries his spirit and is a church community that reflects Shane's character. It really is a church to Enjoy, as I'm sure this book will be—Enjoy!

ALUN DAVIES
Former Senior Pastor of Faith Christian Church,
National Vice President of ACC, Victorian State President of ACC,
National Director of ACCI

Shane Baxter, an apostle sent by God, finally gives us an insight into his journey. As well as overseeing the planting of 170 churches in just a few short years by the movement that he led within his state, Shane shares both the principles that have made his church grow so powerfully and how he has risen from personal challenges that have sadly taken others out.

Personally, I've always been inspired by Shane's humility, enthusiasm and (as his church echoes) joy!

I'm always refreshed hearing from people who have succeeded in their goals, who have overcome impossible challenges and stayed the course through every discouragement. Shane has done all that and more. This book will help impart much of that same joy and grit to you.

PHIL PRINGLE
Founder & Leader of C3 Church Global

ENDORSEMENTS

Shane and Georgie Baxter lead one of the most amazing and impacting churches in the Kingdom. The culture they have curated and created at Enjoy Church is one of the top—if not *the* top reason for their success. Their humility, experience and honest transparency is what makes them beloved throughout their nation and around the world. You would be hard pressed to find anyone like Shane Baxter.

MIKE KAI
Senior Pastor of Inspire Church

Raw, real, practical, authentic, passionate, enthusiastic and ever joyful is my friend and fellow pastor, Shane Baxter.

I have experienced first-hand the culture that has been created at Enjoy and it is one of my favorite places on the planet! The experience is always a little bit of Heaven on Earth.

I encourage you to read on if you want to be encouraged and inspired to dream, and dream again, of what can be possible if you will, "only believe."

PHILLIP O'REILLY
Lead Pastor of The Rock of KC

Shane and Georgie are dear friends to us, and everyone will say they are just REAL people, as do we. Our definition of Real is: **R**aw **E**nergy **A**nd **L**ove.

Shane's accounts of real-life events are inspiring and give us powerful tools to help us embrace the challenges and opportunities that come to each of us, and of course, it's always better to learn from other people's mistakes (tip from my dad).

It's a privilege to have Shane as a friend and partner in the ministry of stewarding God's church here on planet Earth. Shane always brings JOY to the party, even if there is no party. Shane and Georgie, you are always welcome at our table.

MARK AND DARLENE ZSCHECH
Lead Pastors HopeUC. Hope Unlimited Church

ENDORSEMENTS

In these pages you will receive insight, wisdom, strength and encouragement from someone who is not trying to impress you, perform or list accomplishments to gain recognition. Rather you will find someone sharing from a tender, humble and slightly broken heart about how to walk through frustrations, disappointments and emotional challenges. Learning how the truth of God's Word overshadows our weaknesses, embarrassing moments, and thoughts of failure, Shane reveals that God is very aware of our shortcomings. By trusting in His word and His Spirit's leading, we are truly able to guard our hearts and minds and maintain a life of peace and sustained joy.

PASTOR PAUL CHASE
Founding Pastor of New Life Manilla and the New Life Network

Have you ever questioned what God can do through you? We can so quickly discount ourselves from God's plan because we know our imperfections all too well. This book reminds us that God can do anything through anyone He chooses.

Shane shares stories from his life of the journey from being a young carpenter to becoming the senior pastor of Enjoy Church that reveal both his imperfect humanity and God's most perfect grace.

As you follow along with his story in these chapters, you'll most likely see parallels with your own and be reminded that God can and will do exceedingly and abundantly above all that you can ask or think if you Only Believe!

EVAN CARMICHAEL
Senior Pastor Arise Church

I love Shane Baxter. He's fun, he's passionate and he is a brilliant leader. The culture that he and Georgie have created at Enjoy Church is inspirational. It's one of Australia's great churches. In 'Only Believe,' Shane writes as he speaks—humorously, honestly & infused with powerful leadership wisdom forged in the fire of decades of fruitful ministry. You will love the Enjoy story!

JOHN PEARCE
Senior Pastor of C3 Powerhouse, Executive Director of C3 Church Global

ENDORSEMENTS

I will never forget meeting Shane Baxter on a golf course in Southern California. With his towering frame, distinct accent and infectious smile, he greeted me with a warm, "Hello mate!" and I couldn't help but feel an instant connection. Our friendship grew quickly, fueled by our shared experiences as pastors of churches with multiple locations and our mutual dedication to raising children in ministry. Shane is a genuine "fun-monkey" as he likes to say, and one of the happiest people I know. It's not a surprise that the church he leads is aptly named Enjoy!

Shane is humble, authentic, and has the heart of a father. Not only has he shepherded his congregation, but he has also become a spiritual father to countless individuals, mentoring them and fostering their spiritual growth. In this remarkable book, Shane shares insights and principles that have been forged through his own personal journey and years of ministering. Through his relatable storytelling and practical insights, Shane imparts invaluable lessons that resonate with both the seasoned believer and the seeker alike.

What sets Shane apart is his ability to connect deeply with people from all walks of life. His genuine heart for others, combined with an unwavering commitment to the Word of God, enables him to bridge the gap between the spiritual and the practical. As you embark on this journey with Shane, prepare to be challenged, inspired, and transformed as you learn to "only believe."

JARED MING
Lead Pastor of Higher Vision Church

Having known Shane Baxter for nearly thirty years, I can confidently say that he stands alone as one of the most genuine, magnetic, and contagiously joyful leaders you will ever meet. The pages of this book provide a window into his life and the story of Enjoy Church, illustrating his sincere love for people. This is the driving force behind the deep sense of family and generational legacy within his church—two rare traits that can only be attributed to Shane's remarkable leadership.

This book is guaranteed to refresh its readers with honest and transparent stories that inspire world-changing faith to rise in their hearts. Since pioneering Enjoy Church twenty-five years ago, Shane has gifted us with the profound insights documented in this book. It is a must-read for anyone seeking to understand and embody authentic leadership.

SAM PICKEN
Senior Pastor C3 Toronto

ENDORSEMENTS

'What is way more appealing than a filtered reality is authenticity, transparency and integrity.' This phrase, contained in this wonderful book, totally sums up Shane and Georgie Baxter and Enjoy Church. Shane Baxter is an authentic follower of Jesus, husband, friend and church builder. Shane and Georgie have given their lives to build His church, to make Jesus famous and to empower others to step into their personal God adventure. Enjoy Church is one of the premier churches in Australia, impacting thousands of people in fifteen communities in three nations.

You will be blessed, inspired and empowered by Shane's new book 'Only Believe.'

GEOFF AND LEE BLIGHT
Lead Pastors Life Church Brisbane

Contents

Introduction	1
Jars of Clay	4
Joy Comes in the Morning	8
Love Comes to Town	12
It's a Walk of Faith	17
In the Potter's Hands	21
Sent with Blessing	25
The Dream Is Over!	29
Learning in the Valley	34
Wait, Fast, Pray	38
God Will Make a Way	42
Welcome Home	46
Feelings are Overrated	50
We will Reap What we Sow	54
Let's Not Complain About What we Condone	58
Sometimes Crazy is God!	64
Let's Get Comfortable	68
Faith Steps	72
Ask for the Moon	77
Hard Lessons to Learn	82
Broken Hearts and Crumbling Dreams	87
So What's the Point? What's the Point of it All?	91
Culture is King	96
The Wonder Years	101
The Covid Years	108
When Darkness Covered the Earth	112
One Chapter Closes and Another Chapter Opens	118
Acknowledgements	122

Introduction

So how does one begin a book like this? 'Once upon a time' makes it feel like a fairytale. 'In the beginning' makes it sound like a kingdom-tale.

The truth is, I think that either option would be fine as this book is simply committed to advancing the Kingdom of God through ordinary people who are just like us. All the while acknowledging and celebrating the mystery—the mystical and the magical—as to how God weaves His grace and favour through our lives and endeavours for His good will and purposes.

If you've ever doubted your qualifications to do something amazing for God, let me assure you that you're as qualified as anyone is. Whether we are talking about the biblical heroes who shifted the heavens and the Earth in their generations or the heroes of today who go about their ministries changing the spiritual landscapes of this generation. Rest assured, they've all had days where they'd questioned if they had enough; if they would have what it would take.

As I read and listen to many of the 'experts' that I love and respect within the Kingdom of God today, to be honest, at times I am left a little concerned and confused about so much of what is being said. For much of what I hear shouts at my life and says I should never have achieved anything for Jesus or His Kingdom. On the contrary, for the miraculous to be released within the lives of those who fill pages of the gospels, and just for clarification this is the realm in which we want to enter, Jesus said 'ONLY BELIEVE.'

Foolishness to many, I know, but transformational for those who would dare to BELIEVE!

Personally, though, I would tend to think that if you believe that you *already have* what it will take to fulfil your call and purpose, maybe you won't get to see everything God has planned in His heart for your life come to pass. While confidence is a necessity for us all and our confidence is always under attack, it's actually an unwavering confidence in God and His ability to fulfil His will for our lives that we need the most.

I would hope that, as you skip through the pages of this book you will see the miraculous nature of God and the power that lies within a simple faith in Christ and faithfulness to that which He is asking you to do. There is no substitution for clean hands and a pure heart. There's no skirting around the fact that God still desires that we have a heart after His own heart and a basic commitment to walk and live in obedience to Him and His word.

Over the years I've heard and read so much that has intimidated me because it only highlights how unqualified I am. But as I read the stories of men like Saul and David and what it was that qualified them to become the kings that they did, it doesn't seem that they were highly qualified when they were chosen either. Saul's day came when he was out looking for his father's donkeys. David's day came when he was looking after his father's sheep. When Jesus found Peter, he was cleaning his nets on the shore and upon hearing Jesus' invitation to 'come follow Me,' he simply got up and followed. When Peter was in the boat and Jesus said, 'Come,' he simply put his faith in God's Word, swung his leg over the side of the boat and began to walk on water.

Was Peter qualified to walk on the water? Well Jesus thought he was. Were the lads who were out looking after their father's livestock qualified to be kings? Well God thought they were.

INTRODUCTION

So, once again, I hope if you get anything out of this book it's a simple conviction that you're probably way more qualified to do the great exploits that Christ has you to do than you realise.

If you have faith in God and will be faithful to what Christ is asking you to do today, yes, you are qualified, and your tomorrow will get brighter and brighter!

My story has been a simple one and as you'll read, I've just believed. But added to my faith, my life and my story are the most amazing people who have walked out their own faith and stories. Some of these people walked before me, some beside me and some were following behind me.

Many of these people are well-known and familiar. But many are unsung heroes through which the Kingdom of God really does advance. Whether you've played a seemingly prominent role in my life and the story of Enjoy Church, or a seemingly less prominent role, I want to say thank you to you all, for only with you has our story become a reality.

So, grab a coffee, put some tunes on in the background and get ready for God to stir the faith waters of your heart. Yes, you are qualified for such a time as this, so rise up in faith and take your place in history.

Okay, let's do this ...

Jars of Clay

I turned my key in the lock, pushed the door open and stepped over the threshold. Still feeling embarrassed, humiliated and as though I had let the team down, I began pondering the night and what had just occurred.

It was the beginning of the 2015 football season and once again my beloved Tigers had come out against the Blues in the season opener. And as had been the custom for the past five or six years, a bunch of us from church had attended the game, in fact thirty-eight of us had stood together in a crowd of eighty-five thousand cheering on our respective teams.

I was enjoying the night as the second quarter began. Even though we were twenty-three points down, everyone was jovial, and we were all having lots of fun ... *but then!*

Have you ever had a *but then* moment? A moment that you wished could somehow be rewound so you could do it all over again? *But then* ... I heard a 'boof head Blues supporter,' who was sitting two rows behind me begin to abuse a young Tigers supporter who was sitting just a few seats up from me. I turned around to see what was happening and was sad to see that there wasn't just one aggressor sitting two rows back, but five.

I got the young Tiger's attention and simply said, 'Don't worry about them mate. Let's watch the game; let's have a good night and enjoy the game.'

I turned around and continued to watch the game but couldn't help overhearing the 'boof head' continue to rip into the young man. By now my blood was boiling—but I held my tongue (I'm still trying to master this thing called self-control), and eventually the young man and his girlfriend got up and left.

Well, that's the end of that, or so I thought. We were halfway into the second quarter and the Tigers were starting to kick some goals. The Tigers fans were ecstatic, shouts of jubilation filled the Melbourne Cricket Ground (MCG) as the Tigers clawed their way back into the game, and, in the elation of the moment, I shouted out, 'I believe I can fly!'

To most sitting around us it was just a humorous comment that drew lots of laughter, but for the 'boof head Blues supporter', it was as though I had put a target on my back. Within a minute or two, he yelled out, 'I believe you can fly—fly over the balcony!'

Well, I heard it, but I chose to ignore it. Two more minutes went by, and he yelled out at me again, 'I want to see you fly, over the [expletive] balcony.'

Now I've got to tell you I was shocked; I was surprised; I haven't been spoken to like that for years. I asked Gabriel, who was sitting beside me, 'Did he just say that to me?'

To which Gabriel simply said, 'Yep.'

But it's okay, I thought, *I've been a Christian for twenty-eight years now (and I'm mastering self-control), I've just turned fifty, I've got my stuff together, I pastor one of Australia's great churches, I lead the movement that we belong to in the great state of Victoria, I sit on our national executive. I'm a born-again, Spirit-filled, Bible-believing, self-controlled follower of Christ. Sticks and stones will break my bones, but names will never hurt me. You can say what you want, I won't be fazed.*

But then ... he went at me again. This time he said, 'I can't wait to see you fly over the [expletive] balcony.'

Well, I'm not sure what happened to me, and I'm certainly not proud of what happened next, but a sinister dark cloud came over me. I calmly stood up, gave my jacket to Ryo who had arrived from Japan just a few days earlier, turned around and gave the Blues supporter the stink eye.

I said to him, 'All right you've given it to the kid until he's had to get up and leave, why don't you try it with someone your own size?'

He responded, 'I'm just having fun ... and, I want to see you fly over the balcony.'

To which I responded, 'You don't need to see if I can fly over the balcony. Why don't you get up, we can walk downstairs and step outside into the car park and you can see me fly.'

Now I don't know who was more shocked, him, the crowd who was watching all this unfold, or me.

Shane, what are you doing? I asked myself, *Pull yourself together man!*

I gathered my thoughts, cooled my heels, then threw myself under the bus by saying, 'Man, are you going to get up or what? You're all talk. You'll pay out on a kid and his girlfriend until they have to leave but when you get called out you've got nothing to say. Get up, let's go downstairs and let's do this!'

What was I thinking? That Shane had been dead for twenty-eight years, then like the Terminator, out of nowhere, he was back.

I'm glad to say, the 'boof head' didn't stand up, which meant I didn't need to go downstairs. Eventually I turned back around and took my seat. But as I sank into my seat, my heart also began to sink as I remembered that there were thirty-seven other people from church who had just witnessed the entire event unfold.

As I looked across to my brothers, it seemed by the looks on their faces that they were both surprised and a little excited over what had just occurred. But the looks on the faces of their children, particularly their young sons, spoke more of concern and confusion. I'll never forget the looks on the faces of those young boys. Even though they hadn't heard most of what had been said, I knew what I'd said, and I knew I'd crossed lines that night that I never crossed.

So I lay there in bed, on the Thursday night before Good Friday, beating myself up for being an idiot, asking the Lord, 'Lord out of everyone on planet Earth, why would you choose me?' I heard nothing, but it was as though I felt Heaven laugh and, in that laughter, I got my response.

The Kingdom of God doesn't advance through the lives of perfect people, but via broken people, damaged people, strange and peculiar people, people like me who choose to 'only believe!'

So this book is not intended to record accomplishments or to state achievements. It is a book for the very normal majority of us who are a little embarrassed and humiliated by our inner flaws and outward displays of humanity.

My prayer would simply be that by the time you finish reading this book, you will be able to boldly declare; 'If God says it, I believe it. That settles it, flaws and all!'

A THOUGHT TO PONDER

If God was only interested in engaging with perfect people, He would need to start again, but He hasn't done that for He knows His power is perfected in our weaknesses, and when His light and power burst forth from our weak bodies, it's then that He gets all the glory!

Only believe!

Joy Comes in the Morning

It was a Friday afternoon in March 1987—and I was excited because I was about to return to the town where I grew up for the engagement party of one of my close friends. Although I was born in Melbourne, my family had moved to Albury when I was about nine and we had stayed there until I was seventeen. Then, in 1982, the family headed back to Melbourne, insisting we *all* return as a family. Well, they succeeded in taking the boy out of the country but, as many of you would know, they could never take the country out of the boy.

I'm so grateful for my parents. They became Christians not long after we arrived in Albury, so I grew up in the house of God, even though I wasn't necessarily 'of the house of God'.

The alarm went off at 4 am on Saturday morning and we drove to Albury. As I was a long way from God, I was expecting just another big weekend with old friends, catching up and reminiscing about times gone by ... *but then*.

I had heard about God, in fact I'd been hearing of the love and grace of Christ for more than the past ten years, but there's a huge difference between hearing and receiving.

I went to the party, I had a beer, I had two beers—okay, I had more beers than I can remember. In fact, there's much about what occurred on that night that I don't remember, but I can certainly remember the moment Jesus came for me.

After a long night of drinking, I woke the next morning at about 11 am. My lips were burnt and my head was hurting but, in my heart, I was rejoicing at the love and grace that I'd received in the midst of the darkest night of my life.

After shotgunning a dozen or more cans, I was well and truly on my way to oblivion. I remember getting into a scuffle ... I remember being carried to my car ... I remember vomiting out the window down the side of my own car (that's really bad for paintwork, always remove vomit and bird excrement from car duco immediately) ... and I remember being rushed to hospital, placed onto a stretcher and rushed into the emergency ward.

It had been a crazy night. I was well and truly intoxicated and, yes, I had been in and out of consciousness all the way to the emergency cubicle. *But then* ... what happened next would literally change the rest of my life.

In that place, which seemed a little like a zoo, I encountered Christ and His Kingdom like never before. It wasn't actually the first time I'd encountered Jesus. Throughout my teenage years the Lord had reached out to me numerous times, but for my own selfish reasons I had never wanted to surrender to His love.

It was a Saturday night, so the emergency ward was full of crazy people just like me. It was loud; it was noisy; it was a mad house! *But then* ... as I lay there hyperventilating into a brown paper bag, it was like I had entered the twilight zone. In an instant; in a second; in a moment; I could think as clear as clear—as clear as I've ever been able to think. Now that surprised me, but not as much as the realisation that someone had turned the volume off! Say what? That's right, I was lying there and, in contrast to my drunken stupor, I could suddenly think clearly and all the sound had gone. It was like someone in the emergency ward had hit a mute button. I couldn't move, I just lay there.

I can't say that I knew what was happening, but I can certainly say that I knew something was happening *and then* ... He spoke to me.

Out of the silence came a voice, a voice I'd never heard before, but nevertheless a voice that I knew. Out of the silence Jesus spoke to me.

I wish I could say He said, 'The Lord is with you mighty warrior,' or, 'Come follow Me and I will make you a fisher of men,' but He didn't. He simply said, 'If you die now, are you coming to be with Me, or are you going down?' Now at that point in time I was no theologian (probably not at this point either), but I didn't need a teacher, a pastor, or anyone else to explain to me what Jesus was saying.

One of my favourite movies is *Dumb and Dumber*. I love the scene at the end where Jim Carey says, 'So you're telling me that there's a chance.' I understood clearly that God, who is rich in mercy, abounding in grace and lavish with His love, was giving me a chance—a chance that I just knew I had to embrace.

What happened next? Well, to this day, I'm not really sure. I just remember waking up at Rick's place with burnt lips, a sore head and Jesus' words ringing in my head and heart.

All I know is, 'The one who calls you is faithful!' Even when we are unfaithful and faithless, He remains faithful for He cannot deny Himself. When I was broken, rebellious and distressed, it didn't matter how far I ran or where I ran to, it didn't matter how I behaved or what I did, He was there. It was like He was already there, waiting, waiting, waiting for my arrival! *And then* ... He showed me again just how faithful He is.

So I got my burnt lips and sore head out of bed, took some Panadol and, with a sense of excitement like I'd never experienced before, loaded up the ute, (pick-up truck) and headed back to Melbourne.

As I drove back along that road, I knew, I felt, I believed that I was a different man from the one who had driven along that same road only two days earlier, and I knew why I was different. I'd just met my Lord and Saviour. I was a saved man!

Oh, I know what you're wondering, because so was I: Why did I have burnt lips?

A week or so after returning to Melbourne, I rang a mate and asked him, 'Do you know why I had burnt lips after the party?'

To which he replied, 'You burned them while eating the pig on the spit.'

'But that doesn't make sense. Why would my lips be burnt?' I asked.

'The pig was still on the spit!'

'Oh.'

A THOUGHT TO PONDER

Many of us have family, friends, situations and dreams that we have been believing in and praying for. Keep going; keep praying; don't quit. God is at work. He will reward you in due time if you don't give up. I'm so thankful for praying parents and friends who stepped in and used their faith for me when I didn't have a faith of my own.

Only believe!

Love Comes to Town

Upon returning to Melbourne, I just knew what I had to do—I needed to call my good friend Mark Crawford. Over the past year or so Mark had been a great friend, pursuing me even though I did not want to be pursued.

Mark had been my youth leader and someone I'd known and respected for years, so even though I had been trying to get away from church, Mark had been diligently in hot pursuit. Every week, Mark would call me to invite me to Youth, and every week I'd make up another excuse as to why I'd be unable to make it. The only problem was, even when I wasn't following Christ, I never wanted to be a liar, so I would then go off and do whatever it was that I'd said I was going to be doing. Sometimes I'd simply have to go to the movies, other times I would go into Melbourne and dance with the Hare Krishnas. Whatever it was I said I was going to do, that's what I'd do.

I rang Mark and he told me that the youth group was going away to a camp that weekend. I attended the camp, and the rest is history. I will never forget that Friday night when the guest speaker, Ian Fletcher, walked out onto the platform and spoke a word over my life. He drilled me; the Holy Spirit spoke to me, and I was home. Not just back into a relationship with Jesus but I knew that I was meant to be, called to be, designed to be planted in the house of God. Life was awesome!

Oh my goodness, I was alive! I was in love with Jesus, and I was in love with His church. Could life actually get any better? Well, it was about to!

I remember being at supper one Sunday night after church when Mark's sister-in-law said to me in front of everyone, 'You're going to make someone a great husband one day.'

I remember smiling, feeling a little awkward and thinking to myself, *Probably, but I won't be yours*. Ha, I know, you're thinking that I was full of myself. No, we just had a little history.

Not a long history, in fact our history consisted of just one date twelve months earlier. By the end of our three-hour lunch we were on exactly the same page, we never wanted to see each other again. I thought Georgie was a stuck-up snob and she thought I was a cowboy '*yobbo*'. So, by the end of lunch, we were happy to part company and go our separate ways.

So she told me, 'You're going to make someone a great husband one day,' and I was thinking, *but it won't be you*. As she turned to walk off though, my heart gave itself away. It skipped a beat; it skipped a handful of beats!

'No, no, no Lord! Not a girl, not now Lord, it's me and You Lord, we're going to win the world. Lord, I don't want a girl, girls ruin everything Lord, remember Adam and Eve? Lord, I don't want a girl, especially this girl! Don't You remember Lord, we tried this a year ago and it was a disaster, she's a snob, Lord.'

I put my case forward, but it didn't matter. My heart was gone, I was in love, in lust, in deep! Man, how I wanted to win this girl's heart. I was thinking to myself that this was a done deal. After she told me she thought I was going to make someone a great husband one day, she went and told everyone that. Obviously, she was speaking in some kind of futuristic girlfriend code. She was trying to tell me she had the hots for me and that she wanted to make an honest man out of me and have my babies. Ha, how wrong I was!

I soon learned that when Georgie said to me, 'You're going to make someone a great husband one day,' she meant it. But that's all she meant, for she also remembered our very polite and awkward lunch. She recalled walking inside after I dropped her home and saying, 'I'll never go out with that cowboy *'yobbo'* again.' Unfortunately, she remembered as much as I did.

But not being one that's easily put off, I continued the pursuit. These days I'm sure they'd call it stalking and I'd be arrested. Now in context of the day, I broke no laws—but I did pursue. I got people to put in a good word for me, or as many words as they would. I'd happen—just by chance—to be at meetings or places that she would also be at. I'd stick flowers to her car door in the middle of the night with cards asking (begging) her to go to lunch with me.

We started seeing each other casually, but I could tell I was way more into her than she was into me (you're going to make someone a great husband one day ... *whatever*). But still, everything within me was telling me to go for it. I'd ask the Lord if I could walk away, and I was certain I was hearing from Him that she was the girl for me; God's choice for me. But that wasn't what I was hearing from Georgie and my heart was beginning to get weighed down. I have never done rejection well.

Then D-Day came. For some reason we'd been out in Georgie's car, and she was dropping me off home. As she pulled up into the driveway, I asked her how she thought our relationship was going. Well, that was a stupid thing to do! She gave me a bad report. Not as bad as my schoolteachers gave my parents about me, but it was bad. She used terms like, *I don't think ... I don't know ... I don't believe ...* I'm sure you get it. My heart sank and I began to sweat. It felt like I had a pineapple stuck in my throat, so my response was to retreat. I ran inside with my tail between my legs, angry with God. I said to Him, 'I told you this wouldn't work. Girls are trouble, they're a distraction, I don't want to do this anymore. I'm done!' Then I threw myself backwards onto my bed.

But then ... the moment my head hit my pillow I clearly heard the Lord say, 'Faith, Faith, Faith, Faith.' He didn't say what this faith was regarding, but I knew, because instantly my heart was filled with faith in regard to my Georgie Girrrrrl! I would be her Tarzan and she would be my Jane. I would be her Romeo and she would be my Juliet, I would be her Honey Bunch and she would be my Baby, oh yeah. My heart was dancing and I was back in the pursuit of the cutest girl I'd ever seen!

I saw Georgie at a conference the next day and I bounced up to her like I was Skippy the bush kangaroo. She thought to herself, *What do I have to do to get rid of this guy?* But what she didn't know was that God had spoken to me the night before. My heart was set, and I wasn't going anywhere.

We continued to go slow for a couple of months and then I made the mistake of asking that silly question again.

'What are you thinking about this relationship?'

She told me enough for me to want to drop the subject. So I just started talking—not about anything in particular—I just wanted to change the conversation. As I sat there filling the air with empty words, she was formulating in her head how she would tell me this was the last time we would see each other.

And then ... God turned up. While we sat there together in my XC GS Ford Falcon 4.9 litre work ute, the Holy Spirit came and landed on my girl. She told me months later that, as she sat there formulating her farewell speech, the Holy Spirit came upon her. She could feel something like a sheet of peace land on her head, flow down her face and neck and over her shoulders and flow down all the way to her feet. Then she looked at me, still babbling on to fill the air, and she thought to herself: *This is the one.*

Not knowing what had just happened to Georgie in my old Ford, I got out of the car and opened her door. I walked her to her front door and for the very first time drew her close and planted my lips right on hers. Then I said goodbye and walked away like an urban cowboy.

The next time we sat in my car, she said to me, 'Why do I think I'm looking at my future husband?'

She was thinking that because of what the Spirit had revealed to her.

I was thinking, *Man, I must be an amazing kisser—one kiss and now she wants to marry me!* I think we all know the truth; God had had His way.

A THOUGHT TO PONDER

If you're going to walk on water, you will need to be prepared to get wet. I'm not saying you're going to sink, but the breaking waves and sea spray in themselves will at times challenge what you really believe. If you believe, you've got to go for it.

Only believe!

It's a Walk of Faith

The sun was setting, the truck was packed and as the back doors closed, the driver turned and asked for the address to deliver our furniture to the next morning. The very question I'd been avoiding all afternoon—not because I didn't want to tell him—but because we didn't know!

'Ha, are you crazy?' I recall him asking with bewilderment. Well as to whether we were crazy or not, I think that's a question better answered by others, and I'm well aware there were many who thought we were. Although we didn't think so.

Georgie and I had been married for just a year, when I began to get calls at 2 am on Sunday mornings from my friend Rick, who was my childhood best mate. Rick and I met in year 7 and went right through high school together, riding motorbikes, shooting, camping, playing footy and basically having a whole lot of fun and making a whole lot of mischief.

At the time I'd given my heart to Christ, Rick had been living with my family in Melbourne. Along with everyone else he'd seen the change in his best mate, but ultimately it was too much for him, so he packed up and went back to Albury.

So three years later Rick is ringing me at 2 am. To say that he was a little intoxicated when he rang would be a huge understatement. He'd ring and talk about his life, how he was still living the life we all had as teenagers—but we were no longer teenagers—and life for Rick was less than satisfying. I'd sit there in my jocks (Aussie Bonds) telling Rick about the love of Christ and how he could have life and have it to the full. But as Rick would have a skin full (was drunk) it would only be a matter of time before he'd get frustrated with me, tell me to drop on my head (often in colourful language), and hang up.

But then ... one Sunday morning (yep at 2 am) the phone rang again, and this time Rick was different. We talked, and I could tell that he was listening, so I took the opportunity and asked him if he would come to church with us if we came to Albury the next weekend, to which he replied 'Yes'.

Georgie and I had been to Albury together many times, but as we drove into town this time something was different. We couldn't exactly put our finger on it, but within three days our lives would take on another course all together.

On Sunday morning we got up and took Rick off to church. True to his word he was willing to come along, in fact he was excited to come along. I had no idea as we entered that little school hall that the people we were about to meet would soon play such significant roles in our lives and future ministry.

Pastor John preached with conviction, as was his style, then started to give an opportunity for people to give their hearts to Christ. As I looked out of the corner of my eye, I could see Rick was hanging on to every word, and when given the chance, his hand went straight up. Man, what a moment! The joy of the Lord filled Rick's heart and he was alive in a heartbeat.

The fellowship we enjoyed after church with Rick, Pastors John and Marlene, the Simpson family and the congregation was nothing short of beautiful, and so even though it was Rick who was born-again, something came alive in us as well.

As we drove around Albury that Sunday afternoon, we contemplated the possibility of moving there. In the natural this was a silly idea, a silly idea that got both Georgie and I very excited.

Both of our families lived in Melbourne, we both had good jobs in Melbourne, and we had just built our first home there. But our hearts had shifted in a day and were very much arrested by Albury. We dropped in to look at a few homes that were open for inspection, and we tried to find out as much as we could about employment realities in the area, but the most dangerous thing we did was pray. Be careful what you pray.

As we travelled the three-hundred kilometres back down the highway towards Melbourne, we were overjoyed with what had occurred over the weekend. We really didn't want to leave, but as we travelled, we took the opportunity to pray. When driving, an *eyes wide open prayer* is always a good prayer. We simply prayed, 'Lord, if you want us to go to Albury, then sell our house so fast that we couldn't deny that this is your will.' The next day a couple inspected our home, within three days the contracts were signed, and we were on our way. (The house had been on the market for the previous nine months or so with no interest. That was the time of the '89 recession with interest rates at 18%.)

As it usually is, when we started to tell people our plans, our decision was met with a mixture of emotions, ranging from some people being excited for us to other people telling us we were crazy. If I've discovered anything along the way, it's that it is best to have things settled in your heart before making any declarations.

Thirty days later, our house settled, the truck was full of our furniture, and it was time to tell the truck driver the delivery address. Unfortunately, we didn't have one. It wasn't that we hadn't tried to organise a rental by then, it was just that there was nothing available. So we said to the driver, 'Let's pull out at 6 am, and let's believe that by the time we get to Albury, we'll have an address for you.' He looked at us like we were nuts, but he agreed and away we went.

Boy did we pray as we went up that highway. We would pass the truck, pull into the next little town, jump on a pay phone and plead our case to any and all who would listen. As we travelled along the way, we received many knock backs, *but then* ... when we got to Wangaratta which is forty minutes out of Albury, we were given the address of a place to rent. It was in Thurgoona, the suburb where we were planning to attend church. The miracle of this is the fact that the group who gave us this house had knocked us back many times over the month leading up to our move. 'It is against policy,' they said. I guess God's policy trumped their policy on the day. That final forty minutes was by far the best of the four-hour trip!

> **A THOUGHT TO PONDER**
>
> A miracle will never occur as long as your commitment to the comfort of the boat is greater than your desire to obey His voice. But the moment your foot hits the water as you follow His lead, it's then that the miracle occurs.
>
> *Only believe!*

In the Potter's Hands

For me, Albury was saturated with fond memories from my teenage years; for us, Albury was an unfolding adventure. But neither Georgie nor I had any idea what the next five-and-a-half years would do in us.

What were we thinking? I'm not too sure, I honestly can't recall. We just knew that God wanted us in Albury. I think we were concerned for Rick and wanted to make sure he was planted in a good church where he could grow. Other than that, I'm not sure that we were thinking too much at all.

To be honest, I think God got us hook, line and sinker. We knew that His ways were higher than ours and His thoughts were different to ours. But we had no idea as to what He was up to!

Our pastors for that season of life were John and Marlene Simpson. I will always be grateful for this couple; *we* will always be grateful for this couple.

We had been in Albury for about a year, Georgie was working as a receptionist, and I was subcontracting with Rick as a carpenter. (I don't know if you're aware of it but, before I entered full-time ministry, I was a carpenter just like our Lord and Saviour.) We were enjoying church, our new relationships and the country lifestyle.

And then ... one night, after a leadership meeting at Pastor John and Marlene's home, we were walking home around the golf course, and as we walked, Georgie said to me, 'I think you're a leader.'

To which I quickly replied, 'I don't think so!'

But she persisted, 'Think about it. So many of the leadership qualities that Pastor John just spoke about, you possess. Not only that, but everywhere you go people end up following you.'

I said, 'Baby, that's just because I'm having a party and people just want to come along for the ride.' I shrugged off her comments and we kept on walking but in the silence her words rang out loud within my heart.

That truly was a great time for us. Pastor John was a good old-fashioned Pentecostal believer. He believed in the Word of God, and he loved the Spirit of God. He was exactly what I needed. Due to the fact that I'd lived a fairly adventurous life before coming to Christ, I needed someone over me who would love me with a big heart and correct me with a firm hand, and Pastor John did both. I do find it interesting that so many people who attend church today are looking for their pastors to simply be their friends. I thank God that Pastor John was my friend, but he was so much more to me than that. He was my spiritual oversight, my corrector and my coach. He was my spiritual father. Bringing our spiritual leaders down to our common level is a great mistake made by many that will only ever dull or even mute the voice of God in our lives.

So we were in a happy place, our love for Christ was growing and our revelation of Him was deepening. *And then* ... out of nowhere, came the call.

It was the middle of summer and man was it hot! Forty-two degrees Celsius every day. Georgie was working nine to five as a receptionist, and Rick and I were pulling down an old farmhouse. The demolition was well under way, in fact it was chimney time. We had to pull the chimneys down brick by brick. The timber in the old house was worth a fortune, and the clinker bricks were worth over a dollar each. Each day we would begin at 4 am, under lights, trying to beat the heat. Then we'd knock-off (go home) at about midday.

Because Georgie was still at work when I got home, I'd get cleaned up, jump into bed and look to snooze for an hour or so before she got home.

I remember so vividly the first time God called to me. I was in bed; my head was on the pillow, and I was well on my way to a happy place when I heard God speak to me. Not audibly, but powerfully.

He said, 'Get up, go around and tell Pastor John that you're ready for him to prepare you for ministry.'

I could hardly believe how clearly I heard God speak. I was amazed, I was in awe, but I was going to sleep!

The next day exactly the same thing happened, I went to work, came home, got cleaned up and climbed into bed, and when my head hit the pillow, I heard Him again. 'Get up, go around and tell Pastor John that you're ready for him to prepare you for ministry.'

So what did I do? Exactly what I'd done the day before. I went to sleep.

On day three, I got up at 3 am, I went to work, I came home, I jumped into bed, my head hit the pillow and God said, 'Get up, go around and tell Pastor John that you're ready for him to prepare you for ministry.'

And as I had done the previous days, I said, 'Yep,' and closed my eyes.

Then God's voice boomed, 'NOW!' At which point I jumped out of bed, flew around to Pastor John's house, knocked on his door and told him what God had said.

He calmly smiled and said, 'I've been expecting you; I'll see you Thursday afternoon at 4 pm.'

From that Thursday on, every Thursday afternoon at 4 pm I'd meet with Pastor John and one of my peers, Brett Conibear. To say that those meetings were instrumental to my spiritual formation would be greatly understating what would occur over the coming years. I knew that I'd said, 'Lord, have your way in me,' but this— this was intense! There were days when I'd return home feeling as though God had done open heart surgery on me. Both the joy and the pain of those times in Pastor John's lounge room will be with me forever.

A THOUGHT TO PONDER

Greater than what we've done or even what we're doing, God is way more interested in who we're becoming.

God has a plan for you, a purpose for you. It's as uniquely designed for you as you are for it. Recognising those people that God will use to prepare you for what is next in His plan for your life is crucial to you becoming all that you can become. Greater than what you've done, or what you're doing, is who you're becoming. My prayer for all who are reading this book is that we would be as committed to the process as He is!

Only believe!

Sent with Blessing

It was 1994 and life had never been so good! Georgie and I were now parents. Our first daughter, little Emily Pear came into our world the normal way, and my, oh, my, being a dad was and still is the best! (At least it was until our grandchildren arrived.) Georgie and I were loving family life, and our hearts were bursting with excitement for the future.

By then we certainly knew that there was a call to pastor on our lives. We loved the church we were a part of, but there was something more burning on the inside of us. We had always wanted to be the sort of people who stood alongside their pastors, lifting their hands up and doing whatever was required to see the dream that was in their hearts become our reality. But now, when we were dreaming, we were beginning to see something different. That was a little confusing at first, for we loved our pastors, our church and the city God had planted us in. We were in nine meetings a week, five of which either one or both of us led. We did three bump-in and bump-out services on a Sunday, and we were fully committed to the house and the leadership that we were under. But our hearts were beginning to long for a place we hadn't been to and a people we hadn't yet met.

After a long time of prayer and consideration, and with much fear, I really wish I could say with much faith, but we were a little (a lot) intimidated, we went to see our leadership. We told them what was in our hearts. We'd been journeying with Pastor John and Marlene for years, and the truth is we really should have spoken to them first, but as they were overseas on a three-month holiday, in our youthful enthusiasm we thought we would speak to their sons who were the assistant pastors at the time. Hindsight is a beautiful teacher.

Well, the meeting did not quite go to plan, well not our plan anyway. After sharing our hearts with Scott and Glen, we were told that they couldn't see it. Especially at that time! That was because I'd recently asked to be released from one of my weekly responsibilities. Prior to being in nine meetings a week, I'd been in ten, along with working full-time. Scott told us that if we were unable to carry the load that we were carrying, then we wouldn't be able to carry the burden and the demands that came along with pastoring. That was not something we could really argue with as we'd never been senior pastors, so we really didn't know. But the truth is, we never went to see them for an argument, we went in seeking their blessing.

It's in moments like these that we discover whether submission is an ideology, a philosophy or a theological position we actually believe in. We'll never really know if we are submitted, until we need to submit. Many people believe they're submitted when they're simply in agreement. It's only when points of difference come our way that we really discover if we are actually under authority, or just companions travelling in a similar direction.

So what did we do? We made a decision. We decided to love, serve, give and lead with more joy, passion and commitment than ever before. I'm convinced that there will be times in all of our lives where what we believe will be put to the test. Friends, what we do in life always has a counterbalance, what we are doing is important, but how we are doing it is just as important. I'm a great believer that it's the person who is under authority who *has* authority. This spiritual truth is seen as the centurion speaks to Jesus about being under authority and Jesus makes a comment on his great faith. So, for us, to remove ourselves from being submitted under the authority that we knew God had placed us under, was not something we ever considered. The thought of 'wenting' was never an option. We would continue to serve the Lord with gladness in the house that God had planted us in, in the knowledge that if this was God's will for our lives, we could trust that in the fulness of time, we would be 'sent with blessing' and that's exactly what happened.

Twelve months later, I made an appointment for Georgie and I to see Pastor John and Marlene (the people we should have spoken to in the beginning), and truthfully speaking, I was once again a little nervous on the way in, *and then* ...

Pastor John and Marlene were amazing; they sat, they listened, they encouraged us and they prayed for us! As we left their house, we were excited and overjoyed with how well the meeting had gone. Pastor John offered to help me get my credentials with the movement we were in: the Assemblies of God (AOG), now known as the Australian Christian Churches (ACC). He would also introduce me to the state secretary and send us off at the right time with his blessing. 'Wowsa,' what a meeting!

In the following months I obtained my credentials, I was offered a senior pastor position in Melbourne, and we were given a farewell from the church and congregation that had been our family for the past five-and-a-half years.

I remember our farewell from Thurgoona New Life Christian Centre like it was yesterday. I so loved our pastors and was thankful that they would lay hands on us and send us out with blessing. As we drove out of town, down the same road that we'd come in on five-and-a-half years earlier, tears streamed down my face. Tears of grief out of one eye for the friends, church and city we were leaving behind. Tears of joy and happiness out of the other for the life we were about to embrace. If I had known what we were driving towards, maybe there would have been a lot more tears!

A THOUGHT TO PONDER

Songs about crucibles can make for great faith building moments in our worship experiences. But when you feel like you're in one and the heat of Heaven is coming on; when your convictions, beliefs and theologies are being put to the test it's not usually a whole lot of fun. But after your faith has been tested and your heart and motives are seen to be true in God's eyes: *Get ready, get ready, get ready!* I borrowed that last line from the Bishop T.D. Jakes.

Only believe!

The Dream Is Over!

It didn't take long for us to realise we were no longer in the country. We had been living in a nice four-bedroom house on a very generous sized block of land, and now we were in a small two-bedroom unit with no backyard at all. Welcome to Melbourne!

Okay, so our new accommodation wasn't what we were used to, but we didn't come for the accommodation. We were never going to be excited about the accommodation, we were excited about the church and our first Sunday was coming quickly.

Oh man, I was so excited, but I was also nervous! I was thinking to myself, *What have I done? I'm a carpenter* (like our Lord and Saviour, I think I've mentioned that), *what do I know about leading a church, what have I done to my family?* But we were there now, and Sunday was just around the corner.

We arrived a good hour before the service was to commence. Some of the leaders who we had met during the interview process were there. They had the place open, they greeted us, and then we waited for the crowds. Yes crowds. We were believing for the crowds, crowd, anyone. It was about five weeks since we had been in the church for our interview. There had been a great buzz amongst the fifty-or-so people who brought life to the traditional old church building on that day. And this day, as their new pastors, we were so excited to welcome them all back to church.

I remember thinking to myself five minutes before we started the service, *I wonder where everyone is?*

But then ... I looked over to the door as a family of four came in, *here we go*, I thought to myself, but that was it. With those four, we now equated to fifteen people.

I did what I knew to do, and I preached to the multitudes—not the multitudes before me—but the multitudes I was believing for. Once the children's church leaders were taken out (two adults) and the children were taken out (times two) we were left with eleven people in the auditorium. I preached my heart out because at that time I only knew one pace: flat out like a lizard drinking. But even as I preached, my heart was overwhelmed with disappointment at the reality that was before me. We concluded the service, had morning tea and I just had to ask the question.

Grabbing the man who seemed to be the most senior leader of the nine, I asked, 'It seems that two thirds of our congregation are away today, would you know where they are?'

He sort of laughed, then said, 'Oh no Shane, this is it. The day you came for your interview was the day of a baby dedication. Most of the people here on that day were guests.'

To which I responded, 'Oh.'

The next six weeks were a whirlwind of emotions. I felt guilt, disappointment, sorrow and frustration. *What have I done? I've led my wife and two little babies into the desert to die.*

I questioned myself. I questioned my motives. And yes, I even questioned God! I couldn't believe that our dream had so quickly turned into a nightmare. The Love Boat had 'Titanic'd' and we hadn't even left the port.

Now I'm a believer and I have faith, but I'm also fairly realistic. I'm all for storming the gates of Hell, but unless I have a word from God, I'm not going to run at the devil with just a water pistol. And that's exactly how I felt. I felt like I was trying to hose down the flames of Hell with a water pistol—a broken one at that. Please don't misread what I'm saying. The eleven people who made up the church were lovely. There were two Islander brothers who would travel from the other side of the city by train every Sunday morning, not necessarily because they really wanted to be there, but because the previous pastor who was a relative told them they had to be. One of the first things I did was release them and then we had nine. This hurt on a number of levels, but mostly because they were great men who I just loved being with. Our two children's church leaders were brand-new Christians in their sixties. They were lovely, but they were also tired. I don't even know that they really liked children, but they were faithful. As for the rest of the team, they were good people, but this was no church-planting team equipped for the battle that was before us.

Being as pragmatic as I am, I figured if the horse was dead, the best thing we could do was dismount. Just because the horse was dead didn't mean we all needed to die along with it.

In the midst of a very confusing and emotional time, I made an appointment to speak with our state secretary again. This time to speak to him about what we'd just walked into. Pastor Ian is an older, battle-scarred, wise, ministry veteran who understands the complexities of church life. He was very understanding and compassionate in regard to the situation we had found ourselves in, especially in the light that it was the state office that had initially connected us to the church.

When he asked us, 'What do you think you should do?'

I had no hesitation in responding, 'I think we should close it.'

As those words came out my mouth, I was thinking that I was through, and that he would ask for my ministry credential there and then.

But to my surprise he said, 'I agree.'

I nearly fell off my seat. He then went on to ask if we'd be interested in an assistant pastor position back in the country.

I replied, 'Well, it's not as though we'll be busy doing anything else.'

I know—such incredible and inspiring words of faith.

The next day we were sitting at home, *and then* ... the phone rang. The guy on the other end of the line introduced himself as Pastor Mark Bates. He said he and his family were in Melbourne for the day and Pastor Ian had passed on my number in regard to an assistant pastor position.

'Did he now?' I replied.

We spoke for a while then I said, 'Well if you're here, why don't you come over and we'll cook up some spaghetti?' (What I meant was: *Why don't you come over and Georgie can cook up some spaghetti.*)

They came over, and before they had left that evening, we'd agreed to come and have a look at the church and region over the coming weeks.

Before we ventured down to Gippsland, I knew I had to speak to the previous pastor of the church that was in theory now ours. That was certainly the hardest thing I'd had to do in ministry life up until that point in time. They'd given me their baby, a baby that they had birthed and loved, and now I had to tell them I was about to kill it, to close its doors for good. The pastor was confused and sad, his wife was in tears, and I felt like a dog, a very ugly dog at that. But nevertheless, we did what we had to do, and I told them we would be closing the church.

We found ourselves on a trapeze without a net in sight. We were on our way to Morwell AOG for an interview and we had no reason to return to Melbourne. For by then all nine members of the church knew that in just three weeks' time the doors would close for the final time. In hindsight, I'd have to ask myself why we continued on for those following three weeks. Knowing that the horse was going to die, I think we would pull the trigger much quicker today.

A THOUGHT TO PONDER

When God calls us out, the truth is, we will only ever know in part His plans and His purposes in the call. So, if along the way things seem to take a turn, take you in a different direction, don't fear, 'only believe'. Continue on, for the One who promised is faithful. Once the car is rolling it becomes a whole lot easier to steer. Once our faith walk is in motion it becomes a whole lot easier for God to direct our steps.

Only believe!

Learning in the Valley

Well, that seemed positive. I preached, we met the board over lunch and then the job offer was put before me. At first, I was a little taken back as the hours I was expected to work were considerably more than I had been working, and the salary was considerably less than I'd been earning. But, nevertheless, there was an offer, and we had a decision to make.

To be honest, I think God was setting us up, giving us a little heart checkup on the way through. Seeing if we would follow Him out onto the water. The town of Morwell and the region of Gippsland was never an area we would have considered moving to prior to that day. In fact, only three months earlier when the state office had given us the names of a number of places we could possibly plant a church, Traralgon, one of Morwell's sister towns was at the top of the list.

I pulled out my pen and said with a fair level of enthusiasm, 'There's no way I'd ever live there,' and put a line right through Traralgon.

For the record, Traralgon is a great regional city, just not somewhere that I had desired to live. Little did we know that within three months we would be renting in that town and ministering in the town next door. Other than the people we met, there was nothing that attracted us to Morwell. But we really did believe it was a God moment and if we were simply obedient to God, He would take care of the rest.

LEARNING IN THE VALLEY

So with a genuine expectation and excitement for the future we accepted the position. But I did have to tell Pastor Mark something on the way in, and that was simply: 'There's a church in us, so for as long as we're here we'll work hard and do all we can to make you look great, but you need to know, one day I'm going to come to you and ask you to release us.'

To which he said, 'That's fine,' and so we were on our way.

One of the biggest realities missionaries need to deal with when going to and returning from the mission field is culture shock. We may not have gone to the mission field, but we certainly experienced our very own culture shock, both in the church and outside of it. Everything was different for us. It wasn't as though some things were different, no, everything was different. Our senior pastors were as different as chalk and cheese from our previous pastors. The leadership teams were different, the church style was different, ministry expressions and relational connections were all vastly different. Not better and not worse, just different. And the differences really did knock us about for a season.

But once I realised that I didn't actually know everything (that was a revelation) and that what I knew wasn't everything there was to know, we were on our way.

I'm so grateful for the two-years-and-nine-months we served Pastor Mark and Karen Bates and their congregation. For that season certainly helped in our preparation and made us ready for what lay ahead. Well, at least somewhat ready.

Pastor Mark's most obvious gift was administration (he was also a great teacher). My approach to administration was, *don't open the filing cabinet because the devil lives in there*. An approach I soon learned will get you into trouble with the government. But Mark persevered with me and taught me the importance of administration, corporate governance, board affairs, financial management and so much more. I'm sure he questioned at times whether he'd be able to teach this thirty-something-year-old, know-it-all carpenter anything, but I have thanked him and will always thank him for his perseverance.

It wasn't until we'd left Morwell AOG which had been renamed Valley Christian Centre, that I realised it was during those years that my ministry sword was given a second edge. During our time in Albury we learnt the Word. We'd learnt about the person, presence and power of the Holy Spirit. Then during our time in Morwell I learnt about administration, organisation and corporate governance. To be honest, those were things that I was less enthused about but, in the future I would require that knowledge to fulfil Gods plans for our lives and ministry.

One of the other great lessons we learnt during that season was about God's faithfulness. Yes, we believed God to be faithful, we'd heard of His faithfulness, and we'd preached about His faithfulness, but during that time we experienced His faithfulness in the realm of provision like never before.

Friends, God is faithful! You can trust God and bank on His provision when walking in His will. We started on $330 per week. I was used to earning that for a day-and-a-half's work. Now I was the sole provider as Georgie was looking after our girls, but the Great Provider had our backs in the most miraculous ways. During that time, we bought a house, drove a brand-new car and lacked for nothing. We felt like Elijah—who God had the ravens care for. Each day there was always enough for us and for us to show hospitality to any and all who God would bring our way.

One day our accountant rang out of concern for us. He enquired of Georgie, 'Are you guys okay?'

She responded, 'Yes we're fine, why do you ask?'

He said, 'It's just that I know how much you're getting paid, and you shouldn't be able to survive, let alone live like you are. You're not doing anything illegal are you?'

Ha! Praise God, those who trust in the Lord shall never be put to shame.

About twenty months into our new role I found my heart beginning to wander. We were well and truly settled regarding our role and family life. But when I'd go to bed at night, I'd find myself dreaming of a church I'd never seen in a place I'd never been.

We prayed and pondered on this for a while, then we picked ourselves up and went and spoke to Pastor Mark and Karen. Now due to what I had told him on the way into the role, I expected this meeting to be a ten-minute celebration, back slapping, thanks for coming, let's get you on the road and into your own church type of meeting. I can't tell you how shocked, surprised and deflated I was when they told us, 'No, now is not the time.' What da...???

Oh my Lord, what? Not this again? I felt like I was experiencing déjà vu, but I wasn't. This was my life and it was not what I had been expecting!

'So what are we going to do Georgie-Girl?' I asked.

But I already knew the answer to that question before I asked it. I knew the answer because we had convictions, and our conviction was: we'll never just 'went'. We need to be 'sent' because the one who is under authority *has* authority.

A THOUGHT TO PONDER

David may have been obscure to his family and community, but he was never obscure or out of sight to God. He was right where he was meant to be, being prepared for what God had planned for him. *And then* ... a prophet came to town.

Only believe!

Wait, Fast, Pray

We celebrated New Years Eve and welcomed in 1998, a year that would ultimately propel us to a land that God had in store for us.

As we embraced the new year, Pastor Mark and Karen called the church to fast. Fasting was never high on my list of priorities, not because I didn't believe in its spiritual value but, simply because I liked my food! But I heard the call of my leader and followed him into a forty-day fast. What was I thinking? Forty days! That equated to one-hundred-and-twenty meals. I lost twenty kilos (forty-four pounds) and began to look like the grim reaper. Whose idea was this?

Now if I am going to be totally honest, my prayer life during those forty days gained an extra dimension. I was praying for our pastors, I was praying for the church, I was praying for our region and everything that had been put before us to pray for over that period, but still I believed there was a church in us. While we heard our pastors tell us it wasn't time, and we were both willing and wanting to submit to that, we still believed that God was at work in us. We believed He was continuing to prepare us, and prepare what He had for us, so that at just the right time we would collide with our promise and destiny.

Well, forty days passed, and other than people telling me how skinny I looked, I wasn't hearing anything. Anything from my pastors, anything from the state office, anything at all in regard to my extra dimension of prayer life.

What do you do when your expectations fall flat? Just continue to get up with clean hands and a pure heart and serve the Lord by building His church. You'll never go wrong as long as your heart is to build His church!

So, heads down—tails up, let's get on with it. That was a great year, our ministry strength was growing, our relationships were developing, and we were in a great place as a couple and a family.

And then ... I got a phone call, well when I say, *and then* ... I actually mean eight months later I got a phone call. A friend in New South Wales (NSW) called me and asked if I wanted to attend a Church Planters Camp in NSW. Now it was strange and out of the blue that he would call me. He was a friend, but a distant one, and there was no reason in the natural for him to call me. By coincidence, or design, this friend was the same guest speaker who spoke over my life the weekend of the youth camp where I gave my whole heart to Christ in 1987. I'd never said to anyone that I was interested in NSW, and I'd never said that I wanted to plant a church, but for some unknown reason he called, and for some unknown reason the call had got my attention.

The first thing I did was speak to Pastor Mark about attending the camp. He was more than willing to release me for the week to attend, which was very kind. He even said that it didn't need to be holiday hours, but it could be considered work, which was once again very kind. Something was telling me not to accept the offer, as somehow, I knew this invite was connected to my fasting in January and February earlier in the year. That was messing with my head as I neither wanted to live in NSW nor plant a church there. But I decided, *let's just go and see.*

On the first day of the camp, I was told how the week would unfold, which meetings were compulsory and which meetings were optional. And by the way, 'On Thursday afternoon we'll sit with you, look over a map, choose a town and sign you up to plant a church.'

'I don't think so,' I responded, 'I'm just here to learn and seek God in regard to our future.'

'We'll see,' they said.

Monday, Tuesday and Wednesday went by, then on Thursday morning I was sitting in a lecture theatre at our National Bible College, in Sydney, NSW.

I was sitting about eight rows up into the theatre-type seating, minding my own business, which is a miracle all by itself, when God turned up. Now if you're wondering how I knew it was God who turned up, friends, all I can say to you is when God turns up, you know! I began to laugh, I began to cry, I began to say, 'What da!' when this overwhelming presence of love, joy and peace consumed me. I closed my eyes and immediately saw a vision of a blonde woman. (Some of you young guys are thinking, *I've had the same vision!* No, not that vision.) The woman held her three little children close, and it became obvious that this was a broken family. The arm of the Lord stretched all around this family and God said to me as clearly as I've ever heard anything, 'Go back and father your family, church, community and state,' words that were so powerful yet so beyond my comprehension.

When God's presence had lifted and the meeting concluded, I got up and walked straight to the door. As I was about to step through, John, one of the leaders, said, 'Shane, today's the day, we'll speak to you later about where and when you can plant your church.'

I said, 'I don't think so, I've got what I came for, I'm going home.'

'But,' John said, 'It's only Thursday, we still have another day.'

'I'm going home,' I said again.

When I arrived home a day early Georgie asked if I was all right, and I assured her I was. I explained what God had said to me and so that was that. Georgie asked if we were going to follow up the church in Wangaratta as they were looking for a new senior pastor and they'd had our resume for a couple of weeks now.

'No,' I said, 'I don't know what but I'm confident that God is up to something.' And sure enough, He was!

A THOUGHT TO PONDER

It's our responsibility to ask, seek and knock. God's responsibility is to answer, reveal and open. Always remember that while we may be led to pray today, God will respond in the moment, the 'suddenly', and the day that He decides. If you get impatient you may bring an Ishmael into your life. Those who wait patiently for God will enjoy His promises in the fulness of time.

Only believe!

God Will Make a Way

Ten days after returning from Sydney I was at the office and it was just a day like any other day, *and then* ... the phone rang. I answered as I usually did but was surprised to hear it was our state superintendent on the line, I was even more surprised when he said he'd rung to speak to me.

I was surprised because up until then I'd really had nothing to do with Pastor Phil Hills, just a couple of casual encounters where we greeted each other at conferences, but other than that I really didn't know the man.

He started to tell me of a 'broken church' in the western suburbs of Melbourne that he and the state executive thought Georgie and I would be great for. He went on to tell me about the church, but the truth is I didn't really hear much beyond the broken church comment. Ha, looking back on it that's funny! Most people are looking for the dream church, with buildings and cars and staff and finance, but because of what God had revealed to me in Sydney, my heart was leaping over this small broken church.

Pastor Phil was both very kind and encouraging with his words. He suggested that if we were interested, we should make contact as soon as possible and get down to Melbourne for an interview.

Well, first things first, Pastor Phil. Before we could entertain the thought of any interview, we would need to get the blessings of our current pastors. Without Mark and Karen's blessings we wouldn't be going anywhere.

Even though ten or so months had passed since we last spoke to Mark and Karen about moving on to take on our own church, the rejection of our thoughts and desires was still lingering in the back of our minds, so it was with a fair level of nervous anticipation that we entered the room. But, to our surprise once again, they were both very encouraging about us going down for an interview.

Sunday arrived and we found ourselves driving around the western suburbs of Melbourne looking for the Keilor Downs Community Centre.

Oh, that must be it over there, hiding behind the syringe garden! Man, oh man, I've never seen so many syringes.

'Come on girls,' I said, and we grabbed Emily and Maddy and got ourselves inside.

Well, it was what it was, and most of it was average, including my preaching. But what wasn't average were many of the people in that room, people who have become my dearest friends and greatest advocates to this day.

After the service, we made it our endeavour to get to know everyone who had attended. That took a good five minutes and then we headed off to one of the board-members' homes for lunch.

Gihan and Anusha are a lovely Sri-Lankan couple who provided a beautiful lunch for everyone present. Gihan, Peter, Louise and Brother M made up the church board, and although they were all very willing, they, and we, were all out of our depth.

As we began to talk about the church, ourselves, and the possibilities that lay ahead, I quickly realised that one of the board members seemed to be leading the questioning. I had no real objection to him taking the lead, but the manner in which he did it made me want to poke him in the eye. For he was asking questions that neither I nor anyone else could really have answers for.

So we batted backwards and forwards for the afternoon, then thanked them all for their time and agreed we'd speak again in a few days.

As a church and as a board they would need to discuss if they wanted us, and likewise we needed to discuss if we wanted them. One of the challenges, apart from the board member with attitude, was the fact that while they were in a position to pay our salary for the first three months, if we couldn't grow the church in that time then our salary would need to be reduced back to part time.

Georgie and I talked. The truth is we didn't talk much and, as unspiritual as it may sound, we didn't actually pray that much either. It just felt right. It didn't look right, in fact in the natural, it looked completely daunting.

For starters, this church was in the western suburbs of Melbourne, this country boy had never been to the west. This church didn't have a great name; it was called 'Keilor Assembly of God'. Maybe it should have been called 'Killer Assembly of God', as it had had five senior pastors in just a handful of years. You tell me. I was warned this church had its very own 'mafia' and if I was to take the church on, they'd be there to greet me, and sure enough they were. We could go on but what would be the point? In the natural everything was saying 'Danger, danger, danger Will Robinson,' but everything in us was saying 'only believe,' and so that is what we did.

We spoke with Pastor John, who was the current senior pastor, and told him we'd like to put our names up for consideration. The board met, fulfilled their legal obligations, and three weeks later the church voted. We were unanimously elected as the senior pastors of Keilor (Killer) Assembly of God.

Two weeks later, Pastor Mark and Karen would lay their hands on us and send us on to Melbourne with their blessing. A blessing that I'll forever be grateful for, a blessing that has continued to make a path and a way for us even when we haven't been aware of it.

Friends—spiritual principles are spiritual principles. When we think that we have reasons, when we think we have excuses, when we think we're bigger than the ways of God, we'd best think again. Sometimes the best thing we can do for our futures is to pull our heads in and take it to the Lord in prayer. This is not a democracy where everything is nice and neat and fair, no, this is the Kingdom of God. In the Old Testament this Kingdom advanced by way of faith, courage and the battlefield, and in the New Testament it advances by way of faith, courage and righteousness. Whether we like it or not, agree with it or not, God's righteous ways are the right ways and when we adhere to them we'll always get what's been promised!

So, we packed our bags and, just as we had done almost three years earlier, we headed for the western suburbs of Melbourne.

A THOUGHT TO PONDER

As long as you're looking in the natural, you'll be in line for the natural. But when you put your trust in God and allow Him to direct your steps, when you're able to see with eyes of faith and embrace His will for your life, you will see the glorious and miraculous flood your life.

Only believe!

Welcome Home

It's funny the things that you remember. After travelling for almost two hours, we had to pick up some house keys from a family's home. A family who has since become not only good friends, but pivotal in this journey of faith we've been venturing on together.

We were only three minutes from the Battle family home when a concrete truck barreled through a stop sign and nearly took us out. *Welcome to Melbourne, Part Two, Shanee-Boy.*

We picked up the keys from Richard and got re-acquainted with Jan and their two children, Ash and Amanda. Then we headed off to our new rental which was actually the previous pastor's family home.

Okay, before moving on let's do a stock take. On the Sunday of our interview there were around forty people in church, and yes, I did ask if they had a baby dedication, wedding, funeral, bar mitzvah or any other celebration or commiseration that may have inflated the numbers on the day. I was assured the numbers were fairly representative of a typical Sunday. We knew no one on this side of town. We had no family here and we had no friends. We were not familiar with the many nationalities or cultures represented in the western suburbs of Melbourne, but we just knew this was God.

I wish I could say that we knew what we were stepping into, but honestly, we had no idea. I don't say that as a negative, but a mere fact. I'd been an assistant pastor for the past three years, I thought I knew things, I thought I was a man of experience, but really, I had no idea.

As I sit here banging away on this keyboard, a few decades on from when we drove back into Melbourne, all I can do is thank God. The days that lay ahead were to become my greatest place of learning, friendship, love and leadership. I soon became aware that I hadn't necessarily come to build the church, but rather, I'd come to this church that it might build me.

We arrived at our new home, unpacked and bedded down for the night. The next morning, we drove around and ended up in a suburb called St Albans. I had my hair cut in a salon that was filled with Greek girls. They all wore black clothing, talked loudly about the night before at the club, and were mostly called Effie.

From there I stepped out and into the Vietnamese fruit shop next door. I felt like a giant in that place and didn't understand a word that was said. Even though I felt like a total stranger and completely out of place, I also felt a wave of grace flood across my life, and I knew instantly that I was home.

I think one of the dangers we all face when looking for God is that we attempt to seek out what is familiar to us. But familiar doesn't necessarily mean God, it just means familiar. I don't think Moses' burning bush experience was a familiar one, neither was Peter's walking on the water, but they were moments that God was undeniably in. The western suburbs were anything but familiar to us, but we knew we'd discovered our God space.

Over the coming days I made myself at home in the office, which was in a little three-bedroom house on a huge block of land. I pulled the place apart searching for anything that might give me insight into what we'd just taken on. Even though I'm not administrative by nature, I knew the contents of the filing cabinet were going to give me information about the past and help us step into the future. So I went to work and did a stock take.

I wasn't feeling under pressure, but I knew that I only had three months to turn the church around. The previous leadership had made a good investment in a property, which they had sold months before we arrived. Having $140,000 in the bank, I was offered a full-time position for three months, and after that if we didn't break even at the end of each week, I would need to go back to part-time. So let's do this.

As I went through those filing cabinets, I found detailed records of everything since the church was planted in 1986. Every letter written, receipts for every purchase, every board meeting minute, and the names and details for every church member. So, like I said, I wasn't feeling under pressure, but the clock was ticking, and I had a family to feed.

I grabbed the phone list from years past and just started cold calling. I'd introduce myself as the new pastor at Keilor Assembly of God, and then simply let them know that if they hadn't settled in a church since leaving Keilor AOG, I'd love the opportunity to have a coffee with them. Maybe it wasn't rocket science but it was one of the greatest things I ever did. We still have families and friends in church today as a result of those calls.

I finished making calls, worked out the shortfall in our income, tried to work out who was who and the very established pecking order amongst our people, then put my head down and prepared my first sermon as the senior pastor of Keilor AOG. I soon worked out that the title 'Senior Pastor' didn't actually mean that much. I was the only pastor, as well as the chief cook and bottle washer. The only other leadership in the church was our board. It was made up of four inexperienced people, three of whom have become life-long friends. The other swung between brilliant and a pain in the neck until he left (we'll talk about that later).

I soon discovered that what matters more than having a dream to start, is the start itself. I've met so many people who are waiting for the stars to align, their dream ship to sail in, and the team and the finances to all be in place and flourishing before they start. But God responds to faith. Faith is what pleases God and moves mountains. While we do all we can to be well prepared, when you hear God call you out onto the water—just step. Because your step, your faith in action, will be the very thing that will attract the favour of God and all that you need for life and success will be within His favour!

> **A THOUGHT TO PONDER**
>
> Wherever you 'be', be there. Being faithful with what we have is always key in the Kingdom of God to receiving more. While believing for more is good, being faithful and true with what you already have is better.

Feelings are Overrated

There we were, it was Sunday morning, and I was ready to get my 'preeeeach' on, if you know what I mean. I was so excited. Georgie and our girls had never looked so good, my sermon was complete, I was prayed up and ready for take-off.

We pulled into the car park about an hour before the service was to commence, and to my surprise, it seemed as if in the three weeks since we'd last been there, the garden had grown out of control and there were weeds everywhere. As we walked to the entrance of the Keilor Downs Community Centre, I couldn't help but notice again how many syringes littered the garden. It was like a hospital dumping ground for used medical products. I was so mindful that Emmy and Maddy were just five and three years of age, not to mention there were a number of other young families in our church with enthusiastic kids running everywhere. Stating the obvious, it wasn't good.

We entered and were greeted by a small but enthusiastic group of people.

Was it really this loud and echoey when we came here three weeks ago? It was as though we were all yelling at each other, and we were only talking. There was no carpet on the floor, and nothing on the walls to absorb the noise.

Church hadn't even started and already I had some concerns, but it was about to get worse, way worse, because I was about to lead worship. True story. I don't have the best voice; some have said that my singing sounds more like a howling hyena on heat. Personally, I think that's a bit harsh but I'm certainly aware that whatever voice I do have, it has to exit through a pretty rough passage. So I led, Georgie played the three cords she knew on the keyboard and Ash Battle played the base. Yep, that's now Pastor Ash Battle. I'll always remember Ash's father, Richard, who was on the sound desk, giving Ash directions from down the back. That memory all by itself is enough to make me laugh even now.

So we worshipped (just), I preached, I gave an altar call and asked for people to respond to the salvation call—no one did—and then we closed the service.

It wasn't really what I'd imagined. In my imagination I'd always seen a room full of people passionately worshipping along with a full, vibrant, Spirit-led worship team that set the platform up for a preach that would make T.D. Jakes look like an amateur! I'd imagined people on their feet shouting me down as they embraced God's Word followed by an altar call that was full of people giving their lives to Christ. Instead, we had a poor to average first day out, followed by a diversity of welcomes and interrogation by the forty people who called the Keilor AOG home.

But do you know what? In amongst all the sand that was sifted on the day, the truth is I found some gold. Louise Arioka who was out serving in children's church, Peter and Anna Skopilianos who cheered us on then and have continued to do to this very day. Gihan Obeyesekere, our faithful treasurer at the time who has become a faithful friend. Lana Banana, Stephen and Janet, Melva, Brian and Bobby Carmichael and a handful of others. Men and women who saw something they liked and have journeyed with us 'til this very day.

As I drove away that day, I had two very distinct conversations battling away for dominance in my head and emotions. *Mr Underwhelmed* was trying to beat up on *Mr Overwhelmed*. This wasn't the first time these two had gone at it, and it certainly wouldn't be the last.

I was overwhelmed by the sincerity and appreciation I felt by so many in the room, but I was underwhelmed by the reality of what we'd just stepped into! So I had Mr Underwhelmed in my ear telling me all the reasons I should just quit. Between the facility and the lack, Mr Underwhelmed was putting up a pretty convincing case that I didn't have what it would take to turn this church around. It was true I was inexperienced. It was true I had no one to call on. Okay, it was also true I really didn't have any idea as to what to do next, so Mr Underwhelmed had got Mr Overwhelmed in a chokehold on the mat.

But then ... Mr Overwhelmed began to thank God for all the aforementioned people. It's amazing how when you remind yourself of what you do have, your future can begin to look brighter and what you don't have can begin to look smaller. So once again, Mr Overwhelmed got back on his feet and began to remind God of His word to us in Sydney: 'Go back and father your family, church, community and state!'

'That's what You said, Lord, and if that's what You've said, then that's what I'll do! Mr Underwhelmed, you're down and out!'

Well, he was done for then. I had air in my lungs and faith in my heart to face another day.

Two days later Georgie and I would attend our very first ACC (AOG) State Conference as senior pastors. I'll never forget it. We were up the back somewhere, minding our own business again, when the guest speaker from the USA called us forward.

Pastor Wally Odum said to us, 'You're looking at this thing, this church wondering what you should do, what you can do, but understand—it's going to be okay, you're going to have a blast, this ministry is going to be a blast, you're going to have such a blast you will be embarrassed. There'll be times when you won't know what to say, when everyone else will be complaining about how hard the ministry is, you won't know what to say, because you'll be having a blast!'

Well, that was just what we needed to hear, the truth is we already had air in our lungs and a skip in our step, but that word caused us to lift up our eyes and begin to dream. We're ready now, let's do this!

> ### A THOUGHT TO PONDER
>
> Feelings of being underwhelmed, overwhelmed, in too deep, out of control, without hope, despair, etc. are feelings we'll all feel; as men, women, husbands, wives, fathers, mothers, pastors, leaders, business owners or whoever. But the key, and the keys for life will rarely be found in your feelings, rather all the keys for this life and the life to come will be found in the Word of God. What does God's Word say? What has God said? What is God saying?
>
> Only believe!

We will Reap What we Sow

We returned from the conference with our confidence up. Another Sunday came and went, and we enjoyed some good growth from our first week. On our first Sunday we had forty-eight people in church, the second week we had forty-nine. That was a two percent increase! Ha, you've got to take what you can.

I was sitting in my office the following week, and the phone rang. This was the first call I'd received at the office, and I let it ring for as long as I could so I could get my reception and greeting voice on: 'Hello you've called Keilor Assembly of God, Shane speaking.' I nailed it, even if I do say so myself!

Now as this was the first phone call I'd received at the office, I would have loved it if it had been someone looking for a church, someone needing pastoral care, someone wanting to get married or give me a big fat cheque to cover our monthly shortfall, but I certainly didn't expect the call to go the way it did.

It seems that the church we took on had forty people because it had been through a church split, or something ugly like that. It may have been up to one hundred and fifty before the split, but from what I heard the split was pretty nasty and many people had run from the scene of the crime if you know what I mean. Apparently, the church grew when Pastor A brought his congregation in from down the road. Then when he left, he took his previous congregation with him, and many others took the opportunity to flee at the same time, leaving the faithful forty behind. Well, that was the scenario; at least it was until Pastor A called me on that Tuesday morning.

He sounded like a lovely guy, and I'm sure he was a lovely guy, but then he told me that the rental agreement for the Sunday venue was actually his, and in his name, and that he planned to take the Sundays back because he was planning to launch another church. Suddenly I didn't think he was a lovely guy anymore. Truth is, I didn't really know what to think, I'd just got there. *Was what he was saying right? Did he really have the lease? Was it really in his name?* I didn't know. But that wasn't all he was wanting. He also claimed that much of the equipment that was in the rooms at our offices was his as well. Office equipment, musical equipment, and sound equipment. I started going into a cold sweat. 'Lord, what's going on here?' was what I was praying under my breath.

Pastor A provided us with the list of equipment which he believed was his, with the market value of each item alongside it. He was kind enough to say that we could either give him the equipment, or its monetary value. I was shattered and didn't know what to do. It was probably right then that I learned a great leadership ploy; when you don't know what to do—stall—just stall the process and get yourself some time to breathe and think, and of course pray.

Armed with the list of items and their monetary value, I went in search of the facts that surrounded the merging of these two churches. It seemed that when these churches merged, it wasn't really a true merger, it was more like one church absorbed the other. In the years to come we would 'merge' with a number of other churches, but truthfully speaking it's never a merge. We should remove the word merge from the Kingdom and put in another word to prevent unnecessary pain, but we'll leave that for later.

The stall worked, and I gained forty-eight hours of time to breathe and do my homework. Then Peter Skop and I met with Pastor A and one of his elders at the church office. It was a warm greeting, not really like the greeting of an old friend, but nevertheless it was certainly warm. Pastor A then began to paint the picture of what had occurred and had led him to believe that the equipment or its monetary value were rightfully his. Pastor A really was a nice guy, and I have no reason to doubt his sincerity in regard to what he believed and was asking for. He put before me his own list of items, and alongside each item was its value.

So I asked him the question. I may have been shaking in my boots being the new boy on the block, but I asked him the question: 'Are you saying that in the merger, you didn't give the items in question, or the Sunday rental agreement on the building over to Keilor AOG?' He assured me they hadn't. I'm just glad I knew what was in that filing cabinet. Solicitors will typically say: 'Never ask questions in open court which you don't know the answers to,' and there are good reasons why.

To everyone's surprise, I pulled out the minutes that were taken at the time of the merger and put them on the table. If there's one thing the previous pastors were great at, it was administration. All the terms, conditions, gifts and rental agreements of the 'merger' were clearly listed. The rental agreement had clearly been signed across to Keilor AOG and all the equipment had been gifted from one legal entity to the legal entity known as Keilor Assembly of God. Not only was each item listed, but so was its purchase price. As I read out the purchase price against what was being claimed, Pastor A's head began to sink.

That was the moment, when I could put on my face of righteous indignation and tell Pastor A and his elder to, 'Buzz off.' Or I could show grace, the same grace that had been shown to me many times, to my brother in his time of need. Everyone had told me Pastor A was a good guy and I'm sure he was. I'm not exactly sure how or why we ended up having that discussion, but I know it was one that he regretted.

Anyway, this is what I did. I explained my disappointment in what was being asked of me in the light of the real monetary value which he'd signed off on only a few years earlier.

WE WILL REAP WHAT WE SOW

But then I said, 'Regardless, if your cars are out the front, all the equipment you're asking for is in the rooms here, so let's go through the house room by room, find it all and load up your cars.'

Their jaws hit the floor! Then I went on to say, 'And what's more, as you can see you signed that rental agreement over to us, but if you can just give us one more Sunday, the following Sunday you can have that venue, it's all yours.'

I'll never forget the elder's face; tears filled his eyes as he realised everything that had happened in that hour.

When I think about all of God's provision over the years since then, I can't help but wonder, maybe, just maybe in some small way, that that decision to bless Pastor A, even when we didn't have to, has something to do with it. *Don't be deceived, God cannot be mocked, a man reaps what he sows.*

What no one else in the room knew was that earlier in the day I'd been to the local primary school and had organised an amazing deal for our Sunday services. For some reason I found amazing favour with the principal; favour that I'm so thankful for.

A THOUGHT TO PONDER

As you journey through life, with family, in ministry, business, the marketplace, or wherever you are, your values and beliefs will surely be tested. What will matter in these moments isn't actually being right but being righteous. Best you sort out and clarify in your own heart and mind what matters most to you now, because when you're being tested it's too late. We've all seen men and women we know and believe to be good and godly people compromise themselves when opportunity comes to reach for wins or success. It seems foolish to trade our integrity, reputation and godliness for bowls of worldly stew, yet so many do because they've never taken the time to ponder what actually matters most.

Only believe!

Let's Not Complain About What we Condone

I think one of the biggest challenges young and inexperienced leaders face, is simply knowing how and when to wield the authority that they have been given.

If there's one thing that I know I'm not, it's an authoritarian. In saying that, I also know that I'm not one who suffers fools for too long either. Over the coming years I would quickly learn that what I tolerated I condoned, and if I condoned it, I really shouldn't complain about it.

In those first two years we hovered around eighty-five in attendance. It was a crazy time; it was like we were doing a burnout. We were loud, noisy, smoked up and happy, but we were going nowhere. We couldn't seem to move forward. On the surface it looked like we were humming, but underneath we had some very real leadership issues. Issues that at first, I didn't really want to deal with, but ultimately realised that if I didn't embrace the concept of bringing conflict at the right times, then conflict would end up becoming my closest companion and niggling at me for the rest of my life. I shouldn't complain about what I won't deal with.

I don't think anyone goes into leadership because they like conflict, but a leader who doesn't embrace it when required to will end up being owned by it. Generally, leaders won't embrace conflict through fear of loss, but the loss when we don't embrace conflict will always become far greater and wider than it would have been if we had.

At some point in time, every pastor is going to have a wayward board member, a temperamental worship team member or an influential family who behave as though their roots are in the mafia.

Well, within the first three months at Keilor, I realised we had those three leadership realities and just a few more as well.

The only real leadership in the church in the early days was the board. The board were legally responsible for the governance, financial and business realities of the legal entity of the church. Many churches have boards like we have now, made up of men and woman who are qualified and know that they're there to serve the pastors and elders in regard to building a strong healthy legal entity that facilitates the vision of the church. But then there are boards, who are filled with unqualified, ungodly men and women who feel their greatest calling in life is to keep the pastors honest. They see themselves as watchmen on the wall. I see a lot of these people as misguided, ungodly wolves who are often looking for any opportunity to tear the vision and leadership apart for the sake of their misguided pride. These people, while patting themselves on the back, are a constant source of division that keeps the church on the back foot and prevents it from moving forward.

While the board that I'd inherited was not perfect, it was largely a wonderful blessing. Louise Barton, who would soon become Louise Arioka, was and has continued to be an amazing blessing. I refer to Louise as: 'the best friend that I will never have.' I refer to her this way because she is a married woman and I'm a married man, so while Louise might be a great friend of Georgie's and mine, we just draw very clear boundaries to honour our relationship, and the more important covenant relationships that we both have. Peter Skop was another board member, who is still in our church. Peter's friendship and loyalty to me is priceless, and then there was Gihan Obey. Gihan was our treasurer for the first eight or so years, a quiet man with a heart of gold, also still in our church. Gihan is another life-long friend whose company I still enjoy. Then there was Mr M.

Mr M on his best day was a whole lot of fun, and complicated. Complicated is an interesting word that probably doesn't capture what I'm really trying to say, but I'm thinking you can read between the lines.

I remember the day that I was both encouraged and challenged to rise up and start dealing with some of the nonsense that was in our leadership world at that time. Considering that the church is meant to be like a family for godly people, I was thinking someone must have left the back door open. Don't get me wrong, I was happy that we were reaching and bringing people to church that hadn't yet come to Christ, but I expected that by the time someone entered leadership they would have embraced at least some of His character qualities.

Anyway, I remember the night that Mr M's behaviour drove me over the edge, so I asked if I might be able to see him in the kitchen before we left. I also invited Louise in to be a witness for what was about to be said. I called out Mr M on what I said was behaviour unbecoming of a Christian leader. He disagreed with what I was saying.

I said, 'Mr M, you need to realise people are watching you.'

He said, 'Well they shouldn't be watching me.'

I said, 'Mr M, you put your hand up for leadership and now that's part of the cross you bear!'

Well, Mr M lost it, went off tap, had a brain fade, got up and stepped into my space. I honestly thought he was thinking about having a shot at the title. *Let's get ready to rumble* was ringing through my brain.

Then Louise jumped in between us, shoved her finger towards his chest and said: 'You need to sit down and show Pastor Shane some respect!'

Bwaaah, I couldn't believe what I had just seen. The very worst, and the very best of Christian leadership in one moment of time.

Louise had no idea at the time, but when I saw her commitment to stand for godliness in our leadership realms, I was both inspired and encouraged to begin to make the stands that I knew I needed to make myself.

Over the coming months I went after some attitudes in our worship team that had concerned me greatly. The individuals themselves were great young people, but some of them had said to me, 'Creative people are entitled to be temperamental.'

I disagreed. The challenge with temperamental people in any space is that they exhibit characteristics of being half temper and half ..., well, you get the picture. Who wants to, or can, work with that? It's an unhealthy way to do ministry and an unhealthy way to do life. We started addressing what we needed to and soon the team truly began to reflect a worship team.

Then I went after the 'Keilor Mafia'—the family who'd been around since the beginning of time and frankly had far too much influence. Someone once said, 'Keep your friends close and your enemies closer.' I don't actually know who said it but I'm sure it would have been a *Don* someone or other.

I got close to them and closer to those they were influencing. Soon the power shifted as I served and loved the families who'd been bewitched.

The skies above us cleared and became blue, and the oceans calmed, apart from the odd squall that would blow across our bow from Mr M.

Almost two years into our journey we invited a couple of guests to a board meeting. Mr M's behaviour and attitude towards our guests was unacceptable. I was both disappointed and embarrassed at his behaviour. I walked our guests to their cars afterwards and found myself out there apologising for Mr M. Then I walked back in saying to myself, 'It stops here.'

The next morning at 9 am I rang to make an appointment to see Mr and Mrs M at 4 pm. Mr M's wife and children were always a joy, but Mr M's behaviour the previous night broke the camel's back, so to speak.

At 11 am that same day I received a call from the pastor down the road to say that Mr and Mrs M were seeing him at 2 pm to discuss moving their family across.

'Really?' I said.

When they came at 4 pm, they said they felt God was leading them to move on to another church. (Yep, they pulled the God card! Not the 'God told me' card? Yep, the 'God told me' card!)

I said, 'Really? Well, if that's what you feel, I guess we just need to go with that.'

That Sunday, almost two years to the day we arrived, we farewelled Mr M and his family. Don't take me wrong, Mr M wasn't a bad guy, just complicated, and he taught me to realise that I don't do complicated well. The farewell was sincere and honouring.

On just the following Sunday, Tom and Vivien McDonald and their two children came through the door.

It may have been a crazy two years full of challenges, stretching, discomfort and questioning, but I thank God for them because it made me man up and learn what has put me in good stead for the leadership challenges that laid in wait for the years that were ahead of us.

The Sunday that Tom and Vivien came to church, was the Sunday that's still marked in my memory as the Sunday that the church became ours.

LET'S NOT COMPLAIN ABOUT WHAT WE CONDONE

A THOUGHT TO PONDER

Leadership really is a discovery tour. It's the refiner's fire that allows us to discover who we are and what we believe. What we condone, we allow, and if we allow it, we really shouldn't complain about it. If there are attitudes and characteristics within our leaders and those we lead that are at odds with the culture we're trying to establish, we owe it to everyone to have the appropriate conversations to hopefully initiate change. The culture and health of Enjoy Church wasn't established in 2023, it's been twenty-five years in the making, one conversation at a time.

Only believe!

Sometimes Crazy is God!

I will never forget the first time we had one-hundred-and-forty people in attendance at church. We put on a Family Fun Day and added water baptisms just because we could. In those days we would do anything just to attract a crowd—and attract a crowd we did. That little gymnasium was bursting at the seams.

It seemed like a great idea, but not only were we bursting at the seams, we were quickly running out of chairs, so we reached out to anyone and everyone to bring their plastic garden chairs from home—problem solved.

The service was going great. It was a full house, worship went well, the children's item went as well as a children's item can go, everyone who went into the baptismal font came out, and then I got to bring the word.

I'll always remember the moment when I heard what sounded like a crack of lightning as a plastic chair snapped. I just saw the legs of a well-rounded gentleman flying in the air, then heard his back hit the floor. I stopped preaching because of the commotion, and I tried to laugh it off, nervously. He was okay, so someone got him another chair and away we went again. Seriously, no more than two minutes later, 'bang', there went another one, legs were flying in the air and there was another gentleman flat onto his back. So this is what church growth looks like and I was loving it. Can't say I ever saw those gentlemen again; can't say I blame them.

But the sight of that full gymnasium stirred something in me. It was at that point, in early 2000 that I began to believe for a building. I don't think this belief came from a simple cognitive perspective, but from a deep-seated conviction that God was stirring me to begin to believe for His provision regarding our future.

So what did I do? Well, I didn't know what to do so I did all that I could think of doing. And all I could think to do was to grab my good friend Scott and start driving around the western suburbs in search of what God had in mind.

Scott was an elder at that point in time, someone who I had and still have the greatest respect for. An engineer with Qantas, Scott was a line-upon-line sort of guy, someone who dotted the i's and crossed the t's, a man of detail. Looking back and thinking about it I can't believe that he drove around with me on that first Thursday afternoon, let alone nearly every Thursday afternoon at 4 pm for an hour for the rest of the year.

I remember as we were driving around one afternoon Scott said to me, 'So what exactly are we looking for?'

I responded, 'I don't know, keep driving and I'm sure we'll recognise it when we see it.' The truth was I really didn't know what to say so we just drove on.

We drove on week in and week out, but we weren't seeing what we were searching for. Around October that year I grabbed the fifteen or so people that were our core team, set up a whiteboard in our family room and went to work on my presentation. I used a whiteboard because for some reason I thought that I would be more convincing and look smarter if I did so, and it was then that I presented the facts as I knew them.

The price of land in the western suburbs was 'this much', a factory would be 'this much' to buy, and 'this much' to lease. I presented the interest rates, how much money we had in the bank and how much we would need for a deposit if we were to buy, and then I was as honest as I could be.

I said, 'I have no idea what God is going to do, but I have a deep conviction that He is going to provide us with a building, but I don't know where and I don't know when.' My plea was simple, 'Please keep your eyes open and be looking for God's provision, for I know it's coming.'

In January the following year Pastor Nick Resce came and preached for us. Nick was a good friend with a prophetic edge who gave of himself to us in those early days.

As Nick was speaking on that Sunday morning he paused for a moment, and said, 'Shane, God is going to supernaturally and miraculously provide a building for you,' to which I said, 'I know, keep going.' Almost immediately I realised how rude my response may have sounded. That certainly was not my intent. I just knew that what he said to me was a reality, he was prophesying something that I already knew so I wanted him to keep preaching and tell me something I didn't know. He continued to preach and went on his way.

The next day I was out driving around again, by myself this time, looking for God's provision. I found myself standing in someone's half-built factory when I said to the Lord, 'When will you reveal to me where our provision is?' *And then ...* at that moment I remembered a conversation that I had heard the previous Friday.

My first leadership opportunity came by way of serving on the Regional Australian Christian Churches Team (The ACC in Australia, AOG in the USA). The previous Friday we'd had a meeting and one of the agenda items was about an Arabic businessman who was building a church. It was to seat five hundred and would include a children's area, fellowship area, etc. He was looking for a church to use it. In the moment my response was careless: 'Sure he is, whatever, as if someone is going to build a church without a congregation.' I think we all laughed because it sounded ridiculous, crazy, in fact it still does, but what I've come to learn is how often this can sound just like God.

After recalling the conversation, I ran to my car. Still not familiar with all of the western suburbs of Melbourne, I wanted to know where I was, and by chance, I was in the same suburb as the building we'd spoken about on the previous Friday.

First thing on Tuesday I made a call to Pastor Dennis, the pastor who had asked for it to be put on the regional agenda for discussion. He was so glad to hear from me. After hearing of my interest in the property, he made an appointment to meet with Sam Tabban, the owner of the building, the next day.

What happened next was the revealing of God's provision. All these years on I'm still amazed!

A THOUGHT TO PONDER

When you ask, seek and knock in regard to God's provision, don't have God's responses all worked out. We read in scripture how God fed His people by way of the birds and brought resource by way of fish. So why, when we pray and ask for God's provision do we think we have any idea as to how He will bring it. We pray for the miraculous, so let's believe for the miraculous; that's it!

Only believe!

Let's Get Comfortable

Before meeting with Brother Sam, Pastor Dennis thought it would be helpful if he and I met first to talk a little about Arabic culture on the way into the meeting. Being an Aussie who grew up in the country, I was all for meeting with Pastor Dennis because at that point in time I didn't even know what a kebab was.

Pastor Dennis explained to me that what was of more importance than the business itself, was the relationship. 'We have to eat, chat, talk about family and take the time to get to know each other,' he said. It was about then that I realised I must be part Arab for all of that sounded very familiar. Dennis told me that the words we wanted to hear from Sam would be, 'I'm comfortable'. This would be an indication that Sam would be at a place where he would want to talk some more.

Then we went and met with Brother Sam. He is a very sharp, very shrewd businessman who grew up in Palestine. I loved Brother Sam from day one, but he also scared me a little at first if we're being completely honest. We ate, we laughed, we talked about family, football, and the weather, but on the inside, I just wanted to talk about one thing: the building.

Then, finally, he asked me about our church. I was well aware of where Brother Sam's heart was. He had a teenage son who wasn't walking with the Lord, and his heart was very much for youth and the community. So, without exaggerating to the point of lying, I painted the very best picture of our little church that I could and seasoned it all with a desire to reach the young people of our area, which was and still is the truth. After much discussion, many questions and answers, talking and dreaming together, Dennis asked Brother Sam, 'So how do you feel?' Brother Sam said the words I so wanted to hear! 'I'm comfortable,' and then he said, 'Let's go look at the building.'

To be honest, I was so excited I thought I was going to lay an egg. Everything within me wanted to shout, sing, praise the Lord and do a handstand, but instead, I nonchalantly said, 'That sounds like a good idea.'

As Brother Sam walked us through the building, my heart and head were exploding with joy! The opportunity, the potential, the answer to all our prayers, it was all before me. I could see it, touch it, walk through it, and with every step I took, I claimed that building in Jesus' name. As I walked around the mezzanine floor, tears were welling up in my eyes. I couldn't believe what was happening. I couldn't believe that God had prepared all this for us, but sure enough, it really was unfolding before my eyes.

But then ... yes, there was a *but then* that got my attention. I'm a 'let's make it happen, and let's make it happen now' sort of guy. I thought we would go back to Brother Sam's house and seal the deal. *But then* ... as we were walking around the building, Brother Sam said, 'So before we go any further, I need to come to your church on Sunday and see if I'm comfortable.'

What? I thought you said you were comfortable! How many times does a man need to get comfortable?

Then I started to heat up, I had an attack of the sweaty palms as I began to recount what I'd said about our church. Had I exaggerated? Had I blatantly lied about our church? Had I made it out to be bigger and better than it was? I don't think I did, maybe a little, I don't know. But this one thing I knew, I had four days for us to get our stuff together.

I told Brother Sam I would arrange for someone to greet him as he arrived on Sunday, and we all said, 'Goodbye.' Then I went to work.

I don't know that we'd ever worked so hard on a service so that it would come together well. I crafted my sermon for the occasion and for our future. Truthfully it was more vision than reality, but nevertheless I preached it with passion and conviction and the whole church bought in, including Brother Sam.

It was done! We were on our way. *But then* ... yep, another *but then*. We would need to share the building with the Arabic Assembly of God. So now I would need to win their pastor's heart and get *him* comfortable along with the hearts of the Arabic congregation.

Pastor Gaber was an older Egyptian man who was fairly set in his ways. From the time I met him, Pastor Gaber and his wife were very kind to me. At our first sitting they fed us so much food that we thought we were going to explode. After a great time of fellowship, it was obvious, we were all in love.

Now, I thought, *Brother Sam is comfortable, Pastor Gaber is comfortable, I'm comfortable, Jesus is comfortable, so let's do this! No, not yet!*

I was told I needed to go and speak to the Arabic Assembly and make all of them comfortable. *For real?* Absolutely! I dug deep and learned the only Arabic line I've ever learned: 'Ahabakum jamieana,' which simply means, 'I love you all.' As I nervously took the platform, I focused as much as a country carpenter lad could focus and I dropped my line, 'Ahabakum jamieana.' Their eyes lit up as they heard those words come from the mouth of this little Skippy the bush kangaroo. They stood up and applauded and from there, we all just got comfortable together.

At last, the deal was done, and we were on our way.

As we entered the building for the first time, I remember looking across at Brother Sam's confectionary building and saying: 'Lord thank you for this building, but I really want that one over there.' Now before you go judging me and telling me that I was coveting

Sam's building, let me tell you that I absolutely was coveting his building and wanted it badly. I knew we were going to grow, and I knew we would need bigger premises. I wanted his building.

Sure enough, we started growing. Week in and week out we were growing. We had a 10 am service and the Arabic church had an afternoon service. It wasn't long before we were all bumping into each other, and Brother Sam became the referee between our two congregations. Our relationship with the Arabic Assembly was at best challenging. Yes, we respected each other, but it often felt more like we tolerated each other. In spite of that it was working, and we continued to grow.

> **A THOUGHT TO PONDER**
>
> We all understand that a man plans his ways, but it's the Lord who directs his steps. Often leaders are focused on results that are outward for all to see. God is focusing on results that are inward and require us to become more like Christ. Not for a moment would I raise my hand and claim to be the pastor who built Enjoy Church, but I will gladly raise my hand and embrace the fact that Enjoy Church is largely responsible in Christ for building and establishing me.
>
> *Only believe!*

Faith Steps

In 2004 a group of us made our regular pilgrimage to the Edge Conference in Adelaide. With an eight-hour drive each way this road trip was always lots of fun.

We'd always enjoyed the ministry at Edge Conference. Each time, God would speak to us through those who would minister, but this year I was in for a surprise. As I stood there in worship, surrounded by so many, yet all alone in the presence of God, I recall the words that God spoke to me ever so plainly.

By now our church was well over three hundred in attendance yet we still didn't have a youth group. We'd had a few false starts in this regard. We desired to have a youth ministry, but between a lack of youth at church and finding the right leader, it just wasn't happening. As I stood there in the dark on that conference night, He simply said to me: 'If you want to have youth in church then you need to create an environment where youth are going to want to come.' What was funny was that it sounded so obvious. I opened my eyes and looked around. What was screaming for my attention were all the young people who filled the haze filled altar. Above them were moving lights and more speakers than I could count, and so it was that I knew what we were to do.

After the eight-hour drag race back home, we met as a team where I told them what I believed the Lord had spoken to me. I knew what we were to do, and I had some idea as to what it would cost. My plan was simple, paint a picture of the church that I could see to the people, then pass the containers and raise over a hundred thousand dollars! Yep, say it quickly and it sounds feasible; think about it and it's ridiculous. Up until then we'd never raised more than $4000, but we'd been given an opportunity and with opportunity comes responsibility.

I'll never forget the Sunday that I shared what I could see with the church. I painted a picture with my words: of services filled to overflowing, screens on both sides of the platform, and moving lights that cut through the haze as our worship team led us into the presence of God. It sounded a far cry from days in the gymnasium with just four par can lights, but I could see it and so could others.

I couldn't believe the passion, the response, the faith that filled the room. Families came up after the service and said, 'You can count on us Pastor Shane' ... 'We're in'. People were saying, 'We can do more than a hundred grand, Pastor Shane,' and I was saying, 'Yes we can,' but I don't think I really believed.

The following Sunday, as we came to bring our offerings and pledges, by chance we had an apostle visiting from Africa. I'd never met this man before, but he was a friend of a friend who came highly recommended. He lifted the faith in that place to a whole 'nother level! He spoke into the atmosphere like he owned it. The place was ecstatic, we were ready, charged and primed to bring our miracle offering to God. And bring it we did! On the day, $98,000 was given, with another $24,000 coming in over the following week. That day was a day that forged something in our spirits for eternity. If God be for us who can be against us? The apostle preached his message as though he had fire in his bones. As he concluded, he spoke a word over Georgie and me. He said that he saw something in us that he wanted to take to South Africa and France. He said, 'I will make the way, I'll pay all your expenses and take care of all the costs.' I couldn't believe it, just when I thought the day couldn't get any better.

And so it was that we ordered the lights, purchased the hazer, put up the new screens and the place began to fill up. Was that just the result of expenditure and the creation of an atmosphere? No, I don't think so. I think it had more to do with hearing God's voice and being obedient to it, but the atmosphere that was created through the sacrifices of many, sure did help.

It wasn't long before we were pushing five hundred in attendance, so we started a second service. Then we were pushing eight hundred. Three hundred came to the 9 am service, and five hundred to the 11 am service, so once again we had a space issue.

I said to the team: 'I think the Lord just said to me to adjust the times by fifteen minutes, change the services to 9:15 am and 11:15 am, it'll balance up.'

I remember the way the team looked at me when I said that. But I also remember the look on their faces a week later when the congregation spread evenly over the two services, a difference of less than ten between each service.

Those were incredibly exciting days. The church continued to grow, and we enjoyed the favour of everyone. I remember sitting up in the area that we had transformed into our office space one day, saying, 'God what are we going to do? We're running out of space; we're bumping into the Arabic Assembly all the time and that relationship is at breaking point. What are we going to do?' Suddenly a crazy idea popped into my head.

Now I'm not going to say God told me to do the following, but I got up and stepped outside on that cold, rainy, Melbourne day and walked across the carpark to Brother Sam's building. Then I walked around it seven times in the rain claiming it for the work of God. The front of that building was concreted, the back had weeds that were taller than I am, but I pressed through the rain and the mud and found myself going around again for the seventh time. When I got back to the front door, I didn't really know what to do. I certainly didn't shout as I did not want it to fall, so I just walked back across the carpark, cleaned my shoes and went inside as if nothing had happened. But something had happened!

We continued to grow, then we put in a one-hour service at 9 am that we cheekily called Mass. We had a 10:15 am service and an 11:45 am service. By then we had leased some office space from Brother Sam as well as six-hundred-and-sixty square metres of warehouse that we turned into a cafe area. This meant that when people left the 9 am service, they would go for coffee over at the warehouse as the 10:15am service started. Then when that service concluded, those people would go over for coffee and the 11:45 am service would begin and all the while we continued to grow.

By then we were drawing people from all over Melbourne and even beyond the city limits. Truly those were amazing days. With growth challenges on every front, I was having regular conversations with Brother Sam about his building. Brother Sam's heart was knit to us by then, so he was open to the idea, but he also believed it had to be at the right time. I totally understood that, but I found it incredibly frustrating at the same time.

It was during this time that Pastor Mark Connor asked me if I would ever consider doing multisite church; as in planting another campus. I replied, 'No way, I can't do one right, why would I try and do two!'

By the way, the apostle did organise the trip to South Africa and France, and it truly was an amazing experience. In the end he did not pick up all the expenses and costs as he said he would, but that's okay, we just chalked it up to yet another 'learning on the job ministry experience'. It's all good.

A THOUGHT TO PONDER

If you are going to experience growth, you are going to experience challenges. When our girls were children, they would often experience growth pains. Pain isn't necessarily a sign that something is wrong. Often there is a direct correlation between our growth trajectory and our pain thresholds. Being able to understand, navigate and alleviate pain is crucial to our ongoing growth and success.

Only believe!

Ask for the Moon

And so it was that our tenth anniversary came and went. Church had never been better. Discussions were progressing in regard to purchasing our new building. We were also entertaining thoughts of planting our second campus. Not because we wanted to go multisite, but simply out of a desire to minister more effectively to those of our congregation who were travelling over an hour from the eastern suburbs of Melbourne to be with us.

On the horizon I could see a cloud, a cloud the size of a man's fist (sounds like a spiritual line, which I thought would be fitting to get in somewhere).

Now being the Bible scholar that I am, I was aware of what such clouds could represent in the spirit—revival—a Holy Ghost downpour that was going to bring great blessing to us and our church. Well, that must have been the other cloud, because in the fulness of time that cloud would grow into a storm that was going to rip out my heart and kick my butt so hard I'd have puffy eyes for years! Sounds a bit dramatic I know, but it was also pretty accurate. As I have been pondering and considering what this book should or shouldn't contain, I honestly thought about leaving a black hole in regard to those complex years. But that won't help anyone. So I have tried to share in a way that reveals some truths and learnings without being dishonouring towards any individuals in the process. The truth is that up until that time, those were the most challenging and painful days I had experienced in ministry. But as time has passed, I can see that those feelings and emotions probably had as much to do with my own frailty and humanity as they did anyone or anything else.

What I learned in those dark days of leadership was simply how much more growth was required in me. You'll need to wait a chapter or two for a brief glimpse of what occurred. But don't go peeking and don't flick over there now because I am about to give you the account of how we moved into our building and launched our East Location.

By then we were numbering twelve hundred over our three Sunday morning services and bursting at the seams. I was living the dream. We had car park issues, Kidmania issues (children's church), Empire issues (youth group), seating issues and nearly every other issue associated with growth. Our relationship with the Arabic Assembly of God was quickly turning into a basket case because we were growing so fast and stepping all over their toes.

So back to Brother Sam we went. 'It's time Bro, we need to move into the big building before we miss the moment.'

He agreed.

We implemented a strategy that was a blessing to everyone. Brother Sam gave generously to the Arabic Assembly. We as a church contributed to them also and with the savings they already had, they were then able to purchase a building in the northern suburbs of Melbourne and off they went.

Then, as Sam had sold his business by this time, we entered into a twelve-month lease for both of the buildings on his property where we were having church. The lease came with an option to buy in twelve months' time for $4.5 million. If my faith was stretched for the $100,000 for our new generation light and sound show, this would stretch me to breaking point!

Sam would ask me regularly, 'Are you sure you can do this?'

'Absolutely!' I'd respond. But on the inside, I was crying out: *Jesus, help me! Because if You don't, I'm dead, like roadkill dead. Help me Jesus.* And He did.

We ran our campaign and saw the miracle unfold. Now just so you know, I have never really done campaigns well. But, through God's grace and the incredibly generous people of Enjoy, we crossed the car park and entered into our new building. In fact, one Sunday after the service, we all crossed the car park like the children of Israel. We surveyed the building, then placed our hands on the back wall and traced around them with textas. Then we wrote our names and family names inside the lines of our hands. Those traced handprints are on the back wall behind our platform curtain in the West Location to this day.

We got $1.5 million together for the fit-out, invited Pastors Brian Houston and Paul De Jong to speak at our opening, and we were ready to go.

On the day of our opening, I received a text from a good friend of mine, Pastor Enzo Maisano. Enzo was based in the eastern suburbs of Melbourne and was aware that we were looking to establish a location over there. In fact, we'd already leased office space in a warehouse and had a lease agreement for the Sunday use of a local cinema on my desk ready to be signed. So, in the midst of a very busy day, I received his text with words to the effect of: 'You have people in the east, we have a building in the east. Why don't we get together for a blue-sky conversation?'

Needless to say I responded, 'Why don't we!' Even though I didn't really know what a 'blue-sky conversation' was, I knew enough to get the gist of what he was saying.

As we opened our building that night, the auditorium was packed! Pastor Brian prophesied over us and said, 'Ask for the moon,' which is something we've been doing ever since. Then I caught up with Enzo.

We talked about where we were at, where he was at, where Enjoy was at, and where his church was at. The thought of merging our churches together seemed like a great idea to us both.

Over the next six weeks we attended their Sunday services and spent time talking with their board and key leaders. All roads were leading to a 'merger'. In hindsight, as I have said in earlier chapters, I don't think the word 'merger' was probably the right word for the amalgamation of two uniquely individual churches. We've discovered along the way that when people start talking about merging churches, they are often talking about completely different things to what we might be thinking. While I understand the soft and gentle nature of the word 'merger', rarely does it convey what is actually happening. Either in a business or a spiritual sense—and church entails both. Using the word merger, and terms that have similar meanings, while they may make discussions more palatable for everyone at the table, rarely do they convey the reality of what is truly happening. This can often lead to pain and mistrust on the road that lies ahead.

That being said, we continued to meet until finally we came to a place of agreement. At least we all thought it was agreement.

There were a few challenges along the way, but as I look back there will always be one that makes me smile with incredible fondness. Enzo took me to meet Joe Oommen. Joe had been in that church for over thirty years and was a leader with great influence in their congregation. In fact, it was Joe who originally found the building that had become their church home.

I remember sitting there beside Joe on his couch as Enzo tried to explain the benefits of a merger. Well, Joe wasn't having any of it, he was livid, and he didn't mind letting his pastor know. The room was tense, and the atmosphere was heavy and thick. So I looked for my moment to try and defuse the situation.

When Joe stopped to take a breath, I put my hand on his forearm and said, 'You know what Joe?' At which time he looked right at me, but right through me. I continued, 'I have the feeling we're going to become the best of friends.'

Joe simply refocused on Enzo and continued, in no uncertain terms, to tell him what he thought. I love my memory of that day because Joe and I have since become dear friends. I truly love this man and his family and consider him to be an amazing blessing in my life and the life of the church. All of his children and grandchildren are in our church and carry great responsibility in the life of Enjoy Church. Not just in the East Location, but over the whole.

So it was decided: let's do this! We had six weeks stepping it out, before we launched our second Enjoy Location in Mulgrave, Victoria.

A THOUGHT TO PONDER

Always be open to a re-route. In the book of Acts when the church was being birthed, it seemed that the apostles and disciples were always playing catch up. The challenge is, of course, if we're not open to God re-routing us along the way we'll typically stay on the road that we ourselves have mapped out and predetermined is the way. As Proverbs tells us, 'A man's heart plans his way, but the Lord directs his steps.' Therefore, as you journey, be open to the leading of the Spirit, because He will have some roads and laneways prepared for you to travel down of which you're not aware; roads and laneways that will be filled with blessing, friendship and provision.

Only believe!

Hard Lessons to Learn

The agreement that we came to with Enzo when bringing our churches together was that his church would become an Enjoy Church location. Therefore, we would send people and leaders across from the west to the east. He would then go from being the senior pastor of his church to becoming part of the senior leadership team of Enjoy and be based in our West Location, which he did.

But in the years to come I would discover that what he thought was happening may have been different to what I thought was happening.

The truth is, during the initial years of our churches coming together, we caused each other great pain and, although this certainly wasn't intentional from either side, it was undeniable.

When we launched our Enjoy East Location, we had just over a hundred people and six months later we were hovering just under two hundred. Amazing! Except we all know that numbers don't always tell the whole story and that good health is as precious a commodity within the Body of Christ as it is within our natural bodies.

What we were discovering was that these two churches that had in theory just merged, in actuality, hadn't. Well at least not in totality. They had just become two separate Christian entities sharing a building with many of the parts bumping into each other whenever they met. That was how it was beginning to feel.

That was the beginning of the realisation that, even though we all thought we were on the same page regarding values, culture, and DNA, etc, in some regards we weren't even in the same book.

During those early days we simply tried to show grace, even as I'm sure we were also being shown grace.

We were six months into the new season of ministering with two locations and it was like having two girlfriends (not that I'd ever recommend having two girlfriends!) and I found myself very much in love with one and not so much in love with the other.

I still remember going to the USA six months into that new adventure and coming home with a real conviction that I had to address the problem. For if I continued to tolerate it, then I was condoning it.

For the record, there were some beautiful people in our new Enjoy location who are very much part of the fabric and ministry there to this very day. Some were part of the previous church, and some came in over that first six-month period. And there were some beautiful people there who were never going to embrace Enjoy Church, our values or our culture. That didn't mean anything other than our values and focus were different. But to continue together in that way was never going to work long term for any of us. Welcome to our very first round of Culture Wars! I know that sounds combative, but it actually wasn't. We have always had to contend for the culture that's connected to the revelation that we carry of the Kingdom across all of our locations.

We had a senior leadership team meeting where I didn't mince my words. I told our team: 'I'm not loving our new location; I'm not enjoying going there ...'

We were finding that some of the people there who had voted 'yes' to becoming part of Enjoy simply were not willing to embrace our leadership, our people, our values, culture or practices on any level. Some wouldn't even acknowledge those who came across from the Enjoy West Location.

Often the gap between where you're at and where you want to be can only be closed by standing up and embracing some leadership heat. If I had my time over again, I would look for a wiser and more tactful way to have that conversation. I would be way more considered and measured in my words, especially in the light of who was at the table. Sometimes it is not so much what is said, but how it's said.

I was asked the question, 'So what are you going to do about it?'

To which I responded, 'I'm going to shake the tree so hard that anything that's not 'Enjoyable' will fall out.'

And that's exactly what we did! We changed the service time from 10 am to 4 pm. That enabled me to preach there regularly, to speak into the atmosphere and address cultural realities. We removed any leaders we had concerns about, and we painted a very clear picture of Enjoy's values and culture and what it was we were seeking to achieve.

The goal was to create a clear choice for everyone. As such, it enabled those who wanted to come with us to do so, and those who didn't, to feel released to go and find their new home elsewhere within the Body of Christ.

If we thought the first six months were uncomfortable, the next six months just got downright funky! We watched our attendances and finances fall, but truthfully, I could not have been happier, because it was beginning to feel like home! And, after three or four months of discomfort there was a growing sense of unity and it gradually became evident that we were heading in the right direction, even if it had been at a cost.

Then at our one-year anniversary, we held a celebration service. We celebrated, and after the service we had a meeting with the twenty-five-or-so individuals who still weren't wholehearted about being part of Enjoy. We needed to do that as some were having far too many negative conversations around the place, which is not good for any church.

For the next four-and-a-half hours we had an open and frank conversation. On the way into that conversation, I said to the group, 'We can talk for an hour, or we can talk all night, it doesn't matter. But by the end of this conversation, you'll be asked to choose. You can choose to come with us, or you can choose to go from us. If you want to go from us, we'll help you find another church in the area, but we're not doing this anymore!' I then showed them a list of churches in the area with the church names, addresses and service times which we'd printed up earlier that week and we all knew; that was it.

So that conversation alone was one of the most effective things we did to shift the culture in our East Location. At the end of it, a few would be on their way, but that was okay. God has a place for everyone, and for everyone there is a place. Sometimes we just need to help people to find it.

Beyond that conversation it would be true to say that some who were initially unsure, have become champions of the East Location and I'm immensely proud of them and their ongoing contribution to both Christ and His church.

Now just so we're clear, although I don't necessarily think we got it all wrong, neither am I fully convinced that we got it all right. After all, we had never joined two churches before.

We live in a world where, within leadership realms, leaders feel they must be right all the time. Personally, I think there is a great danger associated with such thinking. As I look back to the days when our two churches 'merged', I'm so thankful to Enzo and his wife Helen who trusted us and I am so sorry for any pain that decision brought to them, their family and any others. I am pleased to say that Enzo and I remain friends to this day.

Nevertheless, I do believe that leadership that does nothing in the face of a crisis will almost always end up dead in the water. My recommendation is to contemplate the realities, seek wise counsel, pray to the Lord and act with grace and compassion. That is not always easy in moments of conflict, but it's always the right thing to do.

As time passed, things became good as we began to enjoy peace in the East Location, and the West Location continued humming along.

The year 2010 was the year our State President, Pastor Alun Davies, was planning to resign, and fathering the state, which the Lord had spoken to me about all those years earlier, was becoming a very real possibility.

I remember sitting with Pastor Alun, three weeks before that election and he said to me, 'Shane, be aware that if the presidency comes to you, you're going to come under attack like never before.'

I said, 'Yep,' like I understood what he was talking about. But I had no idea!

If there is one thing that I'm so very aware of now, it's this: If you're taking ground from the enemy, then you're going to become a target for him.

Then in 2010 it happened as the Lord had said and I was voted in as the ACC State President for Victoria. Again, our territory and influence grew. But as our territory and influence grew, so was the cloud that I'd seen on the horizon. *And then* ... six weeks after becoming state president, that storm was about to explode onto the scene.

> **A THOUGHT TO PONDER**
>
> Often when things are being birthed in the natural it can be bloody and painful. Likewise in the spirit it can be the same. The thing that we need to remember as God is trying to reveal something new to us is that people are not the enemy. The enemy is the enemy. Learning how to deal with our own emotions, expectations and realms of conflict will serve us well as we move forward.
>
> *Only believe!*

Broken Hearts and Crumbling Dreams

The joy of ministry is one that I find difficult to explain; the pain of ministry is one that I've found difficult to carry. The point of this chapter isn't about the actions of a few or the faith of the many, the point of this chapter is, 'Who are we becoming?' Or even more so, 'Who am I becoming?'

I think when the sun is shining and the birds are singing, when attendances, offerings, vision and faith are up it's easy to be on your game. But when the squeeze comes on and you feel like your heart is about to burst open, what comes out is really what this chapter is about.

About twelve years into our journey there was a period of time when one of our key couples wasn't doing great in their relationship. It was difficult to watch, to say the least, but it was even more difficult to know what to do. And others were beginning to be impacted by its reality. Truthfully, I don't think I really knew what to do back then. I'd have a much better idea now, but some decisions will always be difficult to make, especially when you know the ramifications will be great and you're not fully aware of all the facts because of the 'smoke'.

With the benefit of hindsight, I would certainly take greater note of smoke in the future because where there's smoke, there's smoke. And no, that's not a typo. There may not necessarily be fire, but if there's smoke there's smoke and that should be enough to set off the alarm bells. I'd also say that when we see signs that alarm us or concern us, not just once but repeatedly, then that's the time to act. Whether we're clear on all the facts or not, it's still the time to act.

Well let's just say that I saw some concerning signs and I did act, but I didn't act strongly enough. My actions should have been stronger.

Out of the blue one day, I received a text from a good friend who was on our board. He wanted to see me immediately, which was unusual, so I made the time and caught up with him a few hours later. The moment he sat down I knew this wasn't going to be pleasant. He looked at me and asked, 'Do you know ...?'

To which I replied, 'No.' But I had a feeling that I was about to find out.

My good friend went on to tell me what he knew. I was devastated. For the record, we're not talking about an affair, but a friendship that was certainly inappropriate. If what was being said was true, and at that point in time I wasn't doubting it was, Hell had just come to town. We sat there together in tears thinking about the very real ramifications that were about to unfold. I'm sure we looked quite a sight to the other restaurant patrons as tears streamed down our faces and into our lattes. Who knows what they were thinking! But it's one moment I'll never forget as our hearts broke over the actions of two people who we both loved. The truth is, I had no idea the extent of the ramifications that would unfold over the coming years as a result.

Even though I didn't know what would happen over the next two years, I knew what needed to happen over the next two days and I was gutted. Not just for my personal loss. But for the loss of the two individuals, the families involved and our church as a whole.

I drove to Pastor Mick and Wendy Reeves' home and cried in the lounge room for half an hour. I then drove home and called Georgie, who had just landed in the Philippines for a mission's trip. She immediately booked the next available flight home which would arrive the next morning. After that I jumped into the shower and cried for another thirty minutes before getting out and pulling myself together to speak to the seventy men and women coming to our home for a leaders' meeting. I probably would have cancelled that meeting except that many leaders were already on their way, so the meeting went on.

Containing my breaking heart, I spoke with as much enthusiasm and faith as I could muster. I was either going to 'faith it' or 'break'. I chose the former. I'm certainly not one who would encourage any minister or preacher to 'fake it', but in that moment I felt if I didn't suck it up and 'faith it' I would soon be on the floor in the foetal position, sucking my thumb. Not a good leadership look.

The next five days were the worst five days in my ministry life up to that time. Yes, I'd been hurt before and yes, I'd been let down before, but this was very different. Never before had I experienced two people so close to me making such poor life decisions. The consequences of those decisions would ripple through all of our lives for years to come.

The following day, based on what we knew to be factual, employment contracts at the church were terminated. But just for the record, if it wasn't for the pivotal roles the two individuals had held within our church, I don't know that the consequences would have been quite so severe.

Then we needed to advise the church. By the grace of God, our national president and good friend, Pastor Wayne Alcorn, was with us as, over that weekend we notified the staff and congregations of our four locations of what we knew, and the actions that had been taken.

To say that time was painful for us all is an understatement. Everyone was gutted. As Enjoy Church has always been a family, the situation was like receiving an arrow right into the heart.

Within a week we had stepped out what we believed were the appropriate actions and were expecting life to return to normal.

What we didn't realise was that what had been the 'norm' for the past twelve or so years would never be the norm again.

> **A THOUGHT TO PONDER**
>
> When my heart broke and parts of our world began to cave in, I thought I was going to die. But I didn't. I thought it was all over. But it wasn't. We're told in scripture that there is a time for everything under the sun, and unfortunately that includes heartache and grief. The challenge for us all is to continue to believe, even when everything we're believing for looks like it's crumbling.
>
> *Only believe!*

So What's the Point?
What's the Point of it All?

Over the next two years, it felt like everything that we had built by God's grace was being loaded into a crucible and sent into the furnace. Every belief, every conviction, every friendship and every relationship was heading into the fire. There were things that we thought were solid over that time that were exposed as weak, and things we thought were true that were revealed as false. From one day to the next surprises were coming from all directions.

Some of the surprises brought warmth, comfort and joy, while others brought more pain and disappointment. People whom we hadn't been sure of proved themselves to be incredibly faithful and loyal friends through this time of trouble. Others who we had thought were family went missing in action and were nowhere to be found.

So what's the point of it all? I think the point of it all can only actually be discovered in the answer to the question: 'Who am I becoming?'

When we think we're the ones building God's church, we are mistaken. While it's true that we have the privilege and the honour of co-labouring with Christ as He builds His church, it is through this activity that God is actually building us. We think we're doing a great work for God, and we are, but the greater work is the work that God is doing in us. And that's the point.

For the ministry is all about picking up your cross and following Jesus. The cross is a symbol of death and it's not until we die that we'll ever truly become like Christ. Obviously, I'm not speaking of a physical death, but a dying to self that removes us from the throne of our own life and positions Christ there in His rightful place as Lord.

In the midst of it all, I had the opportunity to become disappointed and offended; to feel betrayed and abandoned. And I did at times. But I wasn't being crucified. And if I am honest, I think everyone who was part of the team at that time also had the same opportunities, for it was a painful confronting time for us all.

We have a saying at Enjoy Church: 'My heart is my responsibility.' In some ways it's more than a saying, it's a conviction by which we live. We're told in the book of Proverbs that all the issues of life flow from the heart. That's why we need to keep, tend, guard and watch over our hearts above all else. When we watch over our hearts, we're able to fight the good fight of faith and overcome disappointment, offence, betrayal and abandonment when otherwise we might have been overcome by it.

As the months went by and the whirlwind settled, it was obvious that some people were not going to make it. I understand what I understand, but I don't pretend to understand everything. People were hurt deeply, relationships were stretched to breaking point and trust was broken, and each of us had to work it out. What was it all about? It was all about what it's always been about, and that was: Who am I becoming? Yes, the crucible and the winepress are for our benefit. When we yield to God, they will produce in us what He intends, which of course is, the righteousness of Christ.

My greatest challenge during that season of life wasn't the accusations or slander thrown around by the faceless few, but overcoming the feelings being generated in my heart as a result. Always remember that the loudest 'boos' generally come from the cheapest seats.

The Bible tells us that our hearts are wicked, and mine certainly didn't need any encouragement in regard to that truth. So, while I knew that everyone was going through their own grief and sense of loss, I could only do so much for them since my first responsibility was to focus on keeping my own heart right.

Over the next year-and-a-bit our church continued to grow. Although some of our friends decided to go their own way, I wouldn't judge them for their decisions or actions. I'm only responsible for my heart so I need to reserve my judgement for that. The couple who had the relational issues sorted themselves out and have since continued on their way in both family and ministry. The young lady who'd made some poor choices, was as brave as anyone I've ever seen in owning her decisions and rebuilding her reputation and relationships. Needless to say, she has gone on for God and is living a full and blessed life.

What I find interesting about that whole experience is that what I thought had the potential to destroy us, only made our faith, convictions and resolve in Christ stronger and deeper.

Those who worked on their hearts, whatever they chose to do in that season, are not only still in the game but are now literally more effective and fruitful in ministry than they've ever been.

The church, in a moment that I thought might derail us, was both strengthened and encouraged by what they saw in the leadership team in a moment of crisis. We ended up with valuable leadership credit and goodwill in the bank of the people in our church. Partly because of the way we handled the situation publicly, but mostly because of what they observed in us privately. Note to self: everyone is watching, all of the time.

One of the biggest wins to come out that time was my relationship with Pastor Vivien McDonald. Vivvy and her husband Tom had been with us at Enjoy from our second year into the journey, so they were longtime Enjoyers. They had both been instrumental in ministry and our development as a church, but during that time our relationship was certainly put to the test.

If there's one thing that I'm very aware of now it's that I'm not bulletproof. In that first month when things blew up, I think it would be fair to say that I was emotionally punch drunk. I wasn't seeing straight. I was trying to keep my heart right, but I was upside down emotionally and hanging in the fog. With that, I made some wrong assumptions.

Because of the longstanding friendships Tom and Vivvy had with those who were choosing to leave Enjoy, I wrongly joined some dots and incorrectly assumed. Those assumptions in the end would lead to accusations. If I had kept my mouth shut no one would have known what I was thinking. But do you think I could keep my mouth shut? No!

So the assumptions were spoken out. No, let's call it for what it was; the accusations were spoken out. And do you think I did it privately like Matthew Chapter 18 tells us to do? Oh no, I had to do it in front of three others—all key leaders. But whatever, I blew it. I could tell Vivvy was terribly disappointed in what I had to say, but unfortunately, I had no idea at the time how badly I hurt her.

Two months later she stepped into my office and said, 'At some point, we need to talk.'

I said, 'Sure Vivvy, what about?'

She then proceeded to tell me how she had felt when I questioned her loyalty in front of the other team members. I could see in an instant that she was gutted by my accusation, which had stemmed out of my own insecurities. How could I have done this to someone who, for the past ten years, had been nothing but a loyal and faithful friend to me and the church?

I had no excuse. Yes I was emotionally concussed, but that was not an excuse. I was stupid in my thinking and even more so in my actions. And while I knew that I couldn't rewind the time and do it all again, I could humble myself and do what I knew was the right thing to do. I immediately called into the room those three who were in the meeting two months earlier and explained the conversation that Vivvy and I had just had. I then went on, with hat in hand, to give Vivvy the most sincere and genuine apology I think I'd ever given. (Okay, so I've had to apologise more than once in my life, but it was up there.) Just as my heart was my responsibility, so were my actions, and if I had got it wrong, I had got it wrong, and when I got it wrong, I needed to apologise.

Why are leaders so hesitant to apologise when we get it wrong? Everyone knows it when we do, so why not just own it? I've only ever gained respect by owning my mistakes, and that's exactly what happened with Vivvy. I'm not exactly sure what happened in that moment when I gave her my apology. I only know that she extended to me both grace and forgiveness and from that day our relationship became stronger and sweeter than ever.

What's the point? Who's right and who's wrong? Who cares! Who I am becoming is the real point.

A THOUGHT TO PONDER

Our lives are, in part, a relational cross-stitch which is meant to be for the glory of God. There are way greater things to be pondering and hanging onto than, 'Who is wrong and who is right?' What we need to ponder and be reaching for is, 'What would God have me do in this situation?' Only by discovering and stepping out His will may we ever become like Christ. So in the days that you are challenged to the core ...

Only believe!

Culture is King

There is no doubt that we learnt and grew a lot over the first decade of Enjoy Church, and through that learning and growing we were positioned for a wonderful second decade. My encouragement to pastors, business owners, entrepreneurs and newlyweds would simply be, don't despise the learnings of your early years. Yes, you'll experience some challenges and yes, you'll probably fail along the way. But always remember that only those challenges and failures that don't impart valuable lessons are a waste of time. All the rest are actually bitter lemons preparing you for great lemonade.

While many might look at the first decade of Enjoy and chalk it up as being a success, truthfully, it was what was being forged within us, as pastors and as a church, that was our greatest success.

After stepping into our new building in the west we enjoyed our greatest year of growth to date. People started coming from everywhere. Over the next decade we had people coming from around the state, as well as people moving from interstate, specifically to come to Enjoy Church. We had pastors reaching out from around Victoria, Tasmania and South Australia asking if their church could become part of Enjoy. Or in some cases, asking if we would simply take their churches and install one of our pastors.

Those days were filled with *and then* moments. I never knew where phone calls or coffees were going to lead, or what God had in mind for so many of the wonderful relationships we'd developed over the years.

Now that said, one might cynically think they were just wanting to attach themselves to what had the appearance of success. But I don't think so. The reason I say that is because those who came and joined us during those years weren't people who were enamoured by the trimmings or appearances of our success.

And before I go on, don't be fooled by what you see from a distance. In this crazy social media age in which we live, everyone and everything can have the appearance of success. Just as you filter photos before sharing online, businesses, marriages, families, individuals—and dare I say it, even churches—have become great at filtering real life. Pastors are great at this.

For example, 'Let's not show the empty seats in the shot.' Just speaking from experience.

What is way more appealing than a filtered reality is authenticity, transparency and integrity. People are tired of being promised they can have the perfect 'Ken and Barbie' life while all the time struggling with the realities of a plasticised world filled with imitation. This is where the church, and Christians as a whole, really have an opportunity to shine and come into their own, because people aren't looking for perfection. They will take genuineness over perfection any day. In a world where 'over-promising' and 'underdelivering' has become normal, churches, businesses and communities that 'under-promise' and 'overdeliver' are more and more appealing to everyone.

Whenever we've had pastors approach us about their churches becoming part of Enjoy, we've always done our best to take them behind the curtain and show them the other side of what they have seen before having too much conversation. As you stand in many of our Enjoy Church auditoriums and look around, what you see can certainly look impressive. But I've been known to say, 'This room can be likened to the mounting yard at the Melbourne Cup horse race. All the thoroughbreds are in here and everyone looks great.

They're dressed to impress; everything is in place and there are champions everywhere. It even has the smell of success! But don't let this room fool you, for it only reveals one side of our reality. Let's go behind the curtain and check out what I liken to the church abattoirs. For that's where dreams, ideas, ministries and some of our best-intentioned endeavours have gone to die and never been heard of again.'

Sounds dramatic I know. But it's real. And to be honest I think it's one of the great secrets of our success. There are so many people wandering through life who have become disillusioned by all that is fake and covered up by facades. Therefore, when we're honest, real, vulnerable, transparent, genuine, etc—you get the picture—everyone appreciates it.

So, if it's not glossy images of success and promises of instant happiness, what is it that has been so appealing about Enjoy for so many? To answer that, we need to go back to the first decade. It was what was forged in us during those early years. Culture.

Jesus is the original Culture King! His ability to bring and establish culture here on Earth through His life and ministry is why we're enjoying our lives and church so much today. He didn't just reveal to us the way, the truth and the life, but He brought to us a Kingdom that really does have a culture all of its own. Most Enjoyers will tell you that what they love most about their church isn't necessarily the preaching, the worship experience or, for that matter, any of the other great things that we do and participate in as a spiritual family. Rather, it's the culture we imbibe as a church.

What was happening through those earlier years of Enjoy as we wrestled through the challenges, circumstances and the opposition we faced was the forging of our culture. Cultures are established by the teaching and passing down of values and beliefs from one generation to the next. Cultures become ingrained both in families and in churches through the constant endorsing and celebration of belief systems, convictions and unyielding truth. While it's true that during the first decade of Enjoy we had our fair share of furnace and valley experiences, it's also true to say that as we arose from those furnaces and valleys we left with greater commitment and conviction developing within us regarding our cultural values and beliefs.

We have seven core values at Enjoy Church: Relationship, Integrity, Commitment, Excellence, Vision, Faith, and Life, and the reality is, these are just the tip of a very large kingdom iceberg of revelation. When Jesus prayed, 'Thy Kingdom come,' He had ordinary people in mind to establish His extraordinary culture here on Earth, through the way that we walk, talk, live and exist.

Whilst our core values will always be front and centre, they are expressed and established through a much larger body of sayings and phrases that bring what we value and believe into the realms of daily life. As Christians looking to establish a heavenly culture on Earth within our families, churches, businesses, and communities, etc, it's very important that we take what God has revealed to us about Himself and His Kingdom and put words, phrases and sentences around it. In so doing, those who read or hear them are empowered with understanding and enabled to outwork them in their daily living.

Our sayings and phrases might be likened to modern day parables, creating pictures that are easily understood and easy to remember. These sayings and phrases carry both the substance and essence of our revelation of God's Word.

Only a few days ago I had one of the volunteer pastors who is on our preaching roster say to me, 'I find it amazing that the Enjoy Church locations are so far away from each other geographically, and yet in regard to people, atmosphere, faith and love, they're all very much on the same page.' Truly, our culture is key to this.

An essential element to recognise in the success of building culture is that when the culture you're looking to establish gets challenged along the way, as you can be assured it will—sometimes unknowingly and other times very deliberately—it's important that you stand your ground and reiterate the values and beliefs you have. As you do this, you'll give the challengers the opportunity for greater understanding and hopefully a turnaround.

But scripture also tells us that it's not possible for people to walk together unless they're in agreement. And we know this is the truth. So then, if they don't want to turn around, it may be time to cut them loose.

A THOUGHT TO PONDER

How can we tell if we're winning the 'culture war' in our immediate space? I believe that we'll know we're establishing our culture when it's strong enough to be replicated. For culture to be replicated it must be definable, teachable, transferable and able to be imparted. Always remember that when Moses prayed for his leaders, the spirit that was upon him came upon them.

As such, one of my greatest joys has been to watch those spiritual sons and daughters who have been with us for years, move to different states and nations and reproduce the culture of Enjoy Church wherever God has called them to. I love it!

Only believe!

The Wonder Years

Good for you! You've completed twenty-two chapters and you're still with me. I did wonder if the pain, conflict and constant challenge of life and ministry were going to be too much for some. But, if you've made it this far, I have no doubt that you'll be able to see it through to the end.

That said, some might question why I have decided to include some of the more challenging aspects of ministry and leadership. That's an easy question to answer. It's because it is real, and overcoming such realities is often what is required for us to learn, grow and become more like Christ, which of course is the ultimate goal. Sugarcoating the reality won't help anyone. Most of us won't grow simply through reaping bumper harvests. Wouldn't that be a wonderful life? No, most of us grow through the lessons we learn and how we respond while in the presses and furnaces of life.

So these next three chapters are all related to what I have simply called 'The Wonder Years'. I've called them that because they were full of total wonder in regard to the goodness of God and His hand of blessing, even while I was wondering at times, *'What on Earth have I got myself into?'*

In this chapter I want to focus on my years serving on both the state executive and national executive of the movement to which we belong.

I love the ACC. I believe it to be an amazing movement that God has used and continues to use for the furtherance of His Kingdom. And because I believed God had called me to father the state, being on the state executive was the path I needed to take.

I remember the first time I put my hand up for our Victorian state election in 2002. Although I knew it was a path I needed to be on, when people started asking if they could put my name forward, I became more than a little nervous. Not just because of what it would require of me moving forward, but more because I knew that if I was working for the state, I wouldn't have that same amount of time to work on our church. So during this time of contemplation, I needed a word from God. My encouragement to anyone considering ministry, marriage, or any other of life's major decisions is: You need a word from God. 'Why?' you ask. Because whatever is of God may still be sorely tested, but, if you have the foundation of a word from God then you will stand.

I remember getting away down the coast with the family for a few days when one night, at about 1 am, I found myself standing on a bridge in the rain. As I sought the mind of Christ on the matter at hand, He said to me ever so clearly, 'If you build My house, I'll build your house.' Well, that settled it. I didn't need anything else—other than an umbrella. So, I raised my hand as a candidate, the vote happened and ... I lost.

That's right. I lost badly. What happened to 'only believe', you ask? Well, I did believe ... and I continued to believe. I believed so much that, two years later, I put my hand up again at the next election. It reminds me of what one of the psalmists wrote: 'I get knocked down, but I get up again.' Well, that may not be a psalm but it's certainly biblical in concept.

I think it would be fair to say that it was at that election when I realised what I was stepping into. A lot of people in ministry and business end up stepping away from it all because they become disillusioned with people and with the realities of what they are a part of. I'm probably from the opposite camp. I'll happily be 'disillusioned' if need be because who wants to live under an illusion?

It was at the 2004 election when I put my hand up for the second time that a state executive member took the floor just before the vote and put a very pointed question to the conference. He did this because he wanted the election to go a certain way—and it did. Needless to say, I lost again. Welcome to the world where church and politics collide! I don't think his desire was to hurt me personally, but I do remember walking down the road after the meeting had concluded and having an older pastor stop me and, with tears in his eyes, apologise for what had just occurred.

So the illusion was over and I drove back from Geelong to Melbourne with my tail between my legs. I was asked by my friends if I would put my hand up again. People often lose the first time they put their hand up, but it is a rare thing to lose twice, and even rarer for someone to come back around and put their hand up a third time. That said, I believed that I needed to be on that path if I was to father the state, so typically I would say to my friends, 'I've lost twice. I'll put my hand up a third time. But if I lose again, I think that will be it. After all, how much can a koala bear?' A poor attempt at humour to cover my hurting heart.

As it turned out I didn't need to wait another two years. To everyone's surprise, about four months later a vacancy opened on the executive and I received an invitation from our state president, Pastor Alun Davies, to join. For some reason the pastor who had addressed the conference floor at the last election had resigned from the state executive, leaving an open seat at the table. Pastor Alun, knowing my heart to serve the state, invited me to take his place. God works in mysterious ways! Just when you thought there were no more *and then* moments.

Pastor Alun is a wonderful man who would come to play a very crucial role in my life over the coming decades.

So I was off, and sitting at the state executive table. What a treat. I have many fond memories of those early years. I was learning so much—about ministry, about church, about pastors and the ACC. The truth was I had so much to learn, and the Lord had positioned me at this table for exactly that. As the years went by, more and more responsibility came my way.

I had believed that I could father the state simply by being at the table, but Georgie-Girl had always believed that I could only truly father the state by sitting at the head of the table. To be honest, I had zero interest or desire for that. Pastor Alun was my president, my 'small k' king, I loved him and enjoyed serving him. I felt I was making a difference and had no desire to be in his seat. We all know that with the different seats around the table comes different responsibility, and with differing responsibilities comes different weight. I was thoroughly enjoying the level of weight I was carrying in the 'fun-monkey' seat at the other end of the table from Pastor Alun.

But, as time went by, and there was talk of Pastor Alun stepping down from his presidency position, more and more pastors spoke to me about becoming the next state president. It was during this time that I also received a call from Pastor Keith Ainge, the ACC national secretary. He said he was calling on behalf of Pastor Brian Houston who wanted to nominate me for the national executive.

What? Am I on Candid Camera *or something?*

Initially, I respectfully declined and told Pastor Keith of three people who I thought would do a way better job than me. Pastor Keith laughed and said, 'Shane, it's Pastor Brian Houston who wants to nominate you.' I eventually accepted the nomination and, to my surprise, was elected to that table at the next national election in 2009.

So now I was on the ACC national executive which is a completely different deal from the state executive. Then, only six months after being elected onto the national executive, I was elected to be the state president for Victoria. As Georgie had always thought would happen, I was in a position to father the state.

One might think that sitting in rooms with great men and women of God would be altogether wonderful, and those years and the privilege of serving our executives, departments and pastors of the ACC were certainly wonderful. But they also came with their fair share of challenges. I wish I could say that all the relationships made during those years are strong and healthy to this day, but whilst that's largely true, some came with more pressure points than I care to remember.

We need to remember that the ACC is a 'fellowship of autonomous churches'—an oxymoron if ever I've heard one. Our autonomy is in many ways the great strength of our movement, but at times it can also be our greatest weakness. Leading the ACC in Victoria was an incredible privilege. I'll always be thankful for the opportunity to serve the wider church in this way. If I'm honest, it really was way beyond my qualifications, because I don't know that I was ever really qualified to sit at such tables. But then again, maybe I was. I think what qualifies people in God's eyes is very different to what qualifies us in the eyes of men.

When I'm asked about the decade for which I led the ACC in Victoria I often laugh and say that those years were like trying to herd cats—cool and much-loved cats, but cats, nonetheless. Still, the years were also filled with much love and laughter, joy and privilege, ministry and service and I'm grateful for each one of them (years and cats!).

Finally, after twelve years at the national table and sixteen years at the state table—with ten of those as the state president—I knew that it was time for me to step away—but not because I didn't believe in the movement, or what we were doing. On the contrary, what we achieved at the national and state tables during those years was outstanding.

At the national table we effectively navigated a Royal Commission and we returned the movement back to a place of financial health, all the while navigating the daily grind and tensions that arose from the thousands of pastors and thousand-or-so churches across our nation. That was no mean feat.

As a state we planted a hundred and seventy churches throughout Victoria during my ten years as president. While church planting became the responsibility of the state executive during my tenure, the undeniable driving force for us in that space was Pastor Ian Kruithoff. (Good job, my friend!)

But the other truth is that, during these years I ended up with far too much 'blood' on my sword and I was becoming someone I really did not want to become. Between some of the politics and hallway conversations going on around the place, I wasn't just becoming disillusioned, I was becoming disappointed and cynical in my spirit. My time to step away had come.

Now, as you read this, before you get disappointed in me for my honesty, please understand that the overwhelmingly vast majority of people I worked with over these years were, and are, absolutely amazing. But you only need to bite into two or three bad apples and have a few bad experiences before you begin to look at the barrel differently. By now though, it wasn't necessarily the other apples or the barrel that had the issues, it was me. It was time for me to deal with my own heart.

The resounding questions that have always shaped my life and led me in my decision-making are: Who am I? Who do I want to become? And, who am I becoming? We must all determine for ourselves: Are the streams that I'm currently in taking me towards my desired goals, or are they taking me away from them?

My encouragement to you all is to understand that seasons come and seasons go, and there are times and seasons for everything under Heaven. But when the season is over, and the stream begins to take you away from where you want to go, you need to recognise it and have the courage to get out and follow your dreams.

A THOUGHT TO PONDER

If you've been in my leadership sphere you would have heard me say, 'Rarely is the issue the issue.' As Christian, family, business and community leaders, at times we will all find ourselves in places where we can make a difference. Unfortunately, at times we'll also find ourselves in places that we cannot make a difference. Don't allow what is happening beyond the realms of your authority to control what's happening within the realms of your authority. Sometimes we think we have far more influence than we actually do and so we get disappointed when we don't see what we are hoping to see come to pass. If you have the authority, exercise it. If not, let it go. Focus on what you can influence; lead change that benefits everyone; always be light and know when to call 'time!'

Many memories of my years on the executive are absolutely wonderful and, while I might have a few that still challenge me, I remind myself that, at the end of the day, the issue isn't actually the issue. The issue is always me. My heart is my responsibility, so I need to keep it, tend it and guard it with all diligence so that I might always be ready for the next stage of my Kingdom assignment.

Only believe!

The Covid Years

I'm sure most of us would have crazy memories of those years. I certainly do! Far too many. Can you remember when you first heard about Covid 19 and the Corona Virus? I can.

Sitting in a national executive meeting, Pastor Alun Davies began to tell us about a virus that was spreading throughout Asia. Most of us were oblivious to the realities of the virus and some were even jesting around the table about the subject. As a result, Pastor Alun got on a rant and told us all, in no uncertain terms, that this was serious. 'This will impact the whole world, countries will close their borders and the world will stop,' he said.

Sure, they will, I thought to myself in unbelief.

Well, we all know what happened. It happened just as Prophet Alun Davies said it would.

Two weeks later, we were in Cambodia spying out the land with the intention of planting a location there. From there we planned to fly on to Osaka, Japan, to be with our Enjoy location there, when we heard that Australia was about to close its borders.

So instead of flying to Osaka, we changed our tickets and flew directly back to Melbourne. The next day, the Australian borders closed.

The next two years were the most extraordinary years of our ministry lives. They were full of wonder for us all. We experienced the wonder of the church in all of its glory. I'll always be grateful for the people who surrounded us and lifted up our hands during that time.

If you know me, you know that I'm sanguine and 'people time' is what fills my tank. To be confined to our home for a total of fifty-three weeks over the next two years would do things in me that I wouldn't be completely aware of for some time.

During that time, we saw both the best and the worst of people, of families, of church, of leadership, and of governments. The truth is we saw the best and worst of it all. Fear does crazy things in people, but in contrast, faith does great things in people. The stories! Oh, how I wish I had time to tell the stories of all the people who, through faith, were moved to action and became the light and love of Christ to a dark and hurting world.

For me, the incredible wonder of it all was to see the church pivot so quickly. Pivot was definitely a well-used word by everyone during those years, and one that still makes some of us twitch. But pivot was what we had to do.

Family and fellowship are at the centre of Enjoy Church's DNA, but suddenly we couldn't meet. Not only were we not allowed to meet, but our international, state and regional borders were closed. Despite all that, we still had what much of the world didn't: we had faith, and we had love.

I wouldn't necessarily blame anyone in leadership for not getting it right, but some of the decisions being made by many in authority during those years still leaves me speechless. I'm conflicted and confronted as to why people in business were held responsible for their decisions, while people in public office and governments seemed to be exempt from the same. Don't get me started.

But back to Enjoy, my realm of responsibility. I'll never truly be able to celebrate or thank the Enjoy Church family appropriately for the faith and love they exhibited during that time. 'Am I my brother's keeper?' Well as a matter of fact, yes, I am. Thanks for the reminder. Not that we needed to be reminded, but the love, care and ministry that Enjoyers exhibited to each other, and the wider community was one of the most precious things I've seen in ministry.

The church pivoted and within one week we were an online church. I don't believe online church was ever what God had in mind for what might be deemed 'normal' times, but in a time of crisis when the police and military were patrolling the streets, online was awesome.

It was an incredibly difficult time for many. Including me. I hated with a passion being locked up like a prisoner. But I was so proud of the church as she embraced and worked creatively to make the best of the limitations that were being thrust upon us all—church and community alike.

And then ... because we were online, we were able to broadcast across regions, states and nations and into places to which we may never have travelled. I may have struggled, but I'm sure the Apostle Paul would have loved it. Sometimes the best thing we can do is make lemonade from the lemons that life would throw at us. And so it was that we ground it out.

Throughout that season, we saw heroes all around us. We were blessed and encouraged by the video crew, the worship teams, the community teams—who cared for and fed those from both the church and the community—the pastors, the leaders, and the friendship group leaders. There were heroes committing themselves and rising up out of hardship everywhere. And yet at the same time, some felt that God was calling them on.

It was still terrible, with adversity everywhere we looked. I'll never forget the morning one of our neighbours ran out into the street screaming in such a way that I had never heard a mother scream, as her only daughter had taken her life during the night. The pain that I saw in her and the image of the young lady's lifeless body lying on her bed is one that I'll never forget.

The trauma of that season was beginning to grind on me from the inside out. As we went into our sixth lockdown, we had no idea that it was going to last for four-and-a-half months. I wasn't just feeling isolated, but something on the inside of me was crumbling. It was one thing to miss people, but it was a whole 'nother thing to be separated from the people you loved and felt spiritually responsible for. We were not just a church, this was not a casual relationship, we were a family and I was unable to love and care for those for whom I felt responsible. It was killing me.

Then finally, the lockdowns ended. Most of us got Covid at some stage and the church began to come together again as government regulations allowed and our people felt comfortable. Some people left because they felt we didn't do enough, others left because they felt we did too much, but the vast majority came through shining like chosen vessels for the glory of God. Did I mention how proud I was and am of this spiritual family called Enjoy Church?!

And that, of course, is the wonder of it all. I wondered at times during those two years what would be left, but the wonder of it all is that we've come out stronger than ever. God is so good!

A THOUGHT TO PONDER

While so much focus within the Kingdom is given to the promises of God and the good life that's to be had in Him, we must always remember that it's through faith and patience that we inherit what God has promised.

Only believe!

When Darkness Covered the Earth

We welcomed in the year 2022 and the world started opening up again. Everyone was venturing out and trying to discover what the world and life would look like now. I think I was probably like most people—full of hope for the future but carrying something internally that resembled a slimy residue of the covid years.

Years earlier a good friend had told me how he felt when, after losing their family home to a bush fire, he walked through what remained, picking up the fragments that were left. The first months of 2022 were something like that for me. I know this may sound overly dramatic, but that's how it was. In February 2020 we had the best month of Enjoy Church's history. Every indicator that could be measured was up. We weren't just reaching for the moon; we were laying hold of it. Then came the 'fire'.

And then ... we had to work out what was left. To be honest, throughout that year my heart broke many times. Not over lost property or finance, but over people. During those covid years, some of our church family left us. Now I'm well aware that people don't belong to us, but I'm also aware that if we love people the way Jesus loves people, we'll love them with a very open heart. So when people who we'd loved left us, particularly without even so much as a 'goodbye', it hurt. Some of those people had sat at our tables and ministered or served on our platforms for up to twenty-three years, then suddenly they were gone. So, let's just say, 2022 was difficult on my heart.

I remember being asked by my American friends what impact the lockdowns had on Melbournians. The reason I was being asked specifically about those living in Melbourne was because the whole world had been hearing of how heavy-handed the government in Victoria was and how Melbourne was the most locked-down city in the world. I was giving the same answer to all who asked. I would say 'I'm not really sure, I'm not sure anyone knows. But personally, I don't think we'll understand the full impact of the lockdowns and what they have done in us for five to ten years.' Little did I know what was coming my way.

As 2022 continued to unfold I was challenged over and over again. More and more in the second half of the year. But I'm a believer, yeah? 'Only Believe' isn't just a great title for a book, but a great way to do life. With every month that passed, there came another loss, more grief, more heartache and more pain. I felt Christmas couldn't come fast enough as wave after wave was smashing me on the beach of life.

In July, we headed to the USA for a ministry trip. We decided to take a few days' break on our way in and we landed in Mexico to catch up with our beautiful friends, Pastors Phillip and Susan O'Reilly, of The Rock of KC. As we drove to the beach for breakfast, I felt a strange and unfamiliar sickness come over me. It turned out to be vertigo. I think my body was probably trying to tell me something, for just as vertigo made me feel like I was spinning out of control, so it would become a classic picture of what was to come.

Christmas came and went, and we got to the finish line of 2022—just. But we got there. I had a few days off before I was due to travel to Cambodia in early January 2023 for a mission's trip. Pastor Bandith and Bec Nhep had planted our new Enjoy location there during lockdown! They're awesome! They're crazy! Ha! I was so excited to be going to see them, but internally, I was doing somersaults. I was experiencing feelings and thoughts I'd never had before. Darkness was beginning to cover my world.

On the 10th of January I went to see my doctor, Dr Emmanuel Ndukwe. Dr Emmanuel isn't just my doctor, but a personal friend and devoted member of Enjoy. He is also a great man of faith. I entered the room with Georgie and as I took my seat I began to cry. But I didn't just shed a tear, I started to cry uncontrollably. I wish I could say that I had a good cry, got it out of my system and moved on, but that's not what happened. Once I started crying, I cried for sixty-three days straight, sometimes for up to three hours at a time, until I had no strength left to weep.

What I discovered later was there was a natural and physical side to what was happening to me and there was also a very real spiritual side. But we'll leave that for another time.

Five weeks after I began crying, my dear friend and brother-from-another-mother, Pastor Mike Kai from Hawaii (knowing nothing) decided to call for a chat. He called at about 10:30 am our time and I'd been crying for three hours straight by then. When Georgie answered the phone, he was shocked to discover what had been happening. Mike is a dear friend whose wise counsel I'll be forever grateful for. He gave me three pieces of advice, which I followed closely. By that time, I'd been tormented by the worst and darkest thoughts possible, straight from the messengers of Hell.

He encouraged me to:
- Read Pastor Wayne Cordeiro's book, *Leading On Empty*.
- Speak to our key intercessors, Aji and Eni Akintola, who are the leaders of our prayer team and tell them exactly what was happening.
- Speak to a pastor friend of his who has a strong prophetic and deliverance edge to his ministry.

We had been visiting Georgie's family up on the Central Coast, and the next day, as we flew back into Melbourne, I listened to the audio book, *Leading On Empty*.

The book impacted me so much that I couldn't get past chapter one and I cried the whole flight home. I then reached out to Aji and

Eni. I contacted them as our faithful and trusted intercessors, but I was forgetting that they're both highly qualified in the medical fraternity, particularly in the mental health space. That call was life changing.

For over an hour and a half they ministered to me. Firstly, from the scriptures, and then from a health professional point of view. That was the day that God gave His angels charge over me. Not necessarily angelic angels, but His Nigerian angels. At the end of our facetime call they asked if I had someone that I might be able to reach out to for some 'professional' care. You know you're in deep trouble when your intercessors want you to get professional help. I said I wasn't sure, but I was about to call Dr Lekan Ogunleye as I had missed a call from him a week earlier and he'd left a message. The morning he left the message was the morning after the night that I would describe as being my 'night of torment'. It was a night unlike anything I'd ever known before, when I saw and experienced things that I'm not keen to speak about.

After I finished my call with Aji and Eni, I reached out to Dr Lekan. We spoke for an hour and then he said he needed to see me. I guessed that wasn't necessarily a good thing considering my condition. He was going to a conference the next day, but he said he would go late. He opened his office in the morning, and we met for an hour and a half. Long story short: I was diagnosed with severe depression and the long journey out of the valley of the shadow of death had begun.

The reason I made reference to God's Nigerian angels is because our general practitioners (Drs Emmanuel and Vivian), our psychiatrists (Drs Lekan and Ayo), and our key intercessors (Aji and Eni) are all Nigerian. They are God's angels to me, they're my family and I love them.

From there our church family and friends went to work. They cared for Georgie and I in ways that still leave us feeling overwhelmed. I'm aware that many in ministry are kicked to the curb when going through such health challenges, but our experience was the complete opposite.

Our vision team and board worked together to cover and protect us. Conversations were had with Pastor Mike in regard to how our church could best look after us. Pastor Martin Oravec and Pastor Cristian Szust, along with the rest of our incredible vision team and board pretty much led the ship, cared for us, kept the church moving forward and kept everyone believing for the future. We will forever be grateful.

There were so many who reached out to us once they realised things weren't good. People hopped on planes and flew to our aid immediately. Others called and sent text messages of support. I'll never forget those of you who supported us during our darkest hours. We love you. We know who you are.

My encouragement to those who have family or friends who are experiencing mental health challenges is this: don't do it by yourself. If you care for someone who is struggling, you will need support as well. Don't try and do it by yourself because, there's a chance if you do that, you both might end up drowning together.

I'd also encourage those who want to support people with mental health challenges not to feel like you need to fix them. You can't. The chances are you won't always know what to say so don't feel you always need to say something. Words are great, but sometimes a look or a hug, can say it all.

I'll always be grateful for the love and support of my dear brother and friend Pastor Mick Reeves during that time. On his day off he'd pick me up and we'd play golf. I'd often be in tears and talking of my pain and grief. One day I was driving the golf cart down the fairway crying my eyes out when Mick just put his arm around me and said, 'It's going to be okay.' (I love you, my friend.)

I'm also grateful for my friends Dave Vizzari and Ronnie Pozo who were a great support for me during that time. Sometimes I'd drop by Dave's home and just walk straight around the back and into his garage. We'd just sit there and chat, mostly about nothing, then partake of communion while staring at car parts. Then at times the four of us would do pizza on a Sunday night, this was my fellowship over my darkest months as I wasn't able to be in church. I could be there with my brothers, and they were happy for me to say lots or say nothing. Truly brothers are born for times of adversity.

If you're wondering, yes, I did meet with Pastors Mike's friend, who is also a Pastor Mike. There were many takeaways from our conversation, but none more powerful than when he told me how he believed that the enemy wanted my seat of authority and was trying to remove me from it. A reality that would have happened if it wasn't for God's love and support that came through our church and those friends from around the world.

A THOUGHT TO PONDER

Never forget we are not just in a grind; we are in a war. We're not fighting people, but the powers and principalities of darkness. All who are in Christ have seats and positions of authority, and all who are in Christ have an enemy who wants to evict us from those seats and positions. Therefore, as good soldiers of Christ we need to fight the good fight, stand firm, pray like crazy and ...

Only believe!

One Chapter Closes and Another Chapter Opens

Today as I write this, it is the 7th of November 2023, Melbourne Cup Day, and it is heading towards 31 degrees Celsius. I've fallen out of bed and driven around the Western Ring Road towards one of my favourite coffee roasters.

Driving in cars is undoubtedly a happy place for me. Particularly if it leads to coffee. Driving is where I often connect with God and feel His love and kindness shining upon me. As I was driving this morning, I was pondering the past twenty-five years of Enjoy, and the past fifty-eight years of my life. I was pondering the previous twenty-five chapters while contemplating the twenty-sixth, and the last of this memoir.

In and amongst the stories and journey of my life that you've read so far, my prayer for all of you is that as you close this book you've received some takeaways for yourself. Takeaways that will put you in good stead for the seasons and chapters of your life that are still to be lived and written.

While there is much that is uncertain in life, there is much that is truly steadfast and can be trusted and built upon. If you're not familiar with the Bible, I'd encourage you to grab one today. The Bible is God's Word, His letter to humanity. Jesus hasn't left us here on Earth as orphans to try and find our own way through life but has given us His Holy Spirit and His scriptures to guide us through. The Bible is full of wisdom and will ultimately lead us into all the fulness of both this life, and the one to come.

As we read scripture, we can see that it is full of contrast. Black and white and a million shades of grey in between. In reading the accounts and the stories of the men and women of God who fill the chapters and books of the Bible, we can see the dichotomy of the Kingdom of God being outworked on every page. There will always be a struggle. There will always be tensions between light and darkness, good and evil, the spirit and the flesh. Often these tensions reside within us, and just as often they are expressed through our relationships and endeavours. If you have struggles, if you've experienced conflict, if you're still pressing towards that which you believe God has promised you, then you're in good company. For this is what the heroes of faith in Hebrews Chapter 11 were commended for.

Being a Christian doesn't mean that we get to avoid the valleys of life or the heat of the furnaces that will undoubtably come our way. But rather, being a Christian allows us to find the treasure buried in our valleys and bring gold out of our furnace experiences.

I've enjoyed many mountaintop moments, but there is always another valley to be traversed before one can ascend the next mountaintop. And yes, I've witnessed amazing things, but there was often a furnace that I had to pass through on the way to seeing them.

My encouragement to you all is not to despise the furnaces of life. For if you despise the furnace, you will rarely take from it the joy that is there to be had. Who knows, maybe you will even discover Jesus in the furnace in ways that you've never seen Him or known Him before. Have you ever thought about why David said, 'Though I walk through the valley of death,' and didn't say, 'Though I run through the valley?' Most of us would run from Death Valley, but not David.

David was a shepherd, and he knew that even though he was in a place he didn't want to be, he was with *his* Shepherd, and it would be okay. David knew that if he walked and talked and listened to his Shepherd, he'd glean and learn wisdom for life that would not just bring him through but would set him up for the seasons and chapters to come.

In just a few minutes' time you'll close this book and get up to live the rest of your life. Could it be that, as you close this book you might also close out this chapter of your life, and ready yourself for another chapter? Maybe chapter two, the greatest chapter of your life? The chapter that chapter one was preparing you for?

For me, 2024 doesn't just represent the turning over of a new calendar year, but the opening of a brand-new chapter of my life. Every page of my life has brought me to this place where I might once again ask myself, 'Who am I? Who am I becoming? Who do I want to become?'

It is only through the conflict of our experiences, the contrast of relationships, the contradictions of life and contesting with God that we'll ever truly be able to answer the questions that shape us most.

I need to own some realities in order to answer the questions and navigate the realities of the previous two paragraphs. If my heart truly is my responsibility, then I need to be responsible for the condition of my heart, therefore:

- I need to work on my marriage and family relationships
- I need to work on my health (physical, emotional, and spiritual)
- I need to work on my self-awareness
- I need to remain planted in a Bible-believing/teaching church
- I need to continue to make myself accountable to others
- I need to forgive and let some things go
- I need to humble myself and remain teachable
- I need to love and lay my life down for God, as well as others
- I need to look to the future with eyes of faith
- I need to believe that the God-ordained plans and purposes for my life are already being woven into chapter two.

ONE CHAPTER CLOSES AND ANOTHER CHAPTER OPENS

To those we love and have been loved by,
To those we have helped and been helped by,
To those we have shared our lives with and have received so much life from,
Thank you.
And see you in the pages of ...
Chapter Two

Acknowledgements

It's only appropriate that I take a moment to thank those without whose help this book would never have been completed.

To my wife Georgie, thank you for eight years of encouragement and initial editing support. You have been faithful and true beyond anyone else in my life. Thank you for believing and always being prepared to step with me. I'll love you forever and a day!

To my parents and sisters, thank you for the love and the home that I had the privilege of growing up in. Mum and Dad, you are the best!

To my children and grandchildren, you fill my heart with love, joy and expectation for the future.

To all the pastors in my life who have helped me and shaped me along the way, thank you—particularly Pastor John Simpson and Pastor Glen Berteau.

Sue Marshall, thank you for taking on the official editing role and bringing so much knowledge and guidance to the table.

Ruth Vizzari, thank you for your encouragement and commitment to seeing the book completed.

Mike Kinsman, Pastor Cristian Szust and Nico Tapia, thank you for your support during the book project and its cover design.

Thank you to all of my friends, near and far who have encouraged me for years in regard to writing this book.

Finally, thank you Jesus for this most beautiful life that's filled with beautiful people, love, joy, peace & kindness.

www.ingramcontent.com/pod-product-compliance
Lightning Source LLC
Chambersburg PA
CBHW062038290426
44109CB00026B/2662